The *Grammar* *Handbook*

Dee C. Konrad
Pamela B. Adelman

Good Year Books

An Imprint of Pearson Learning

® Good Year Books
are available for most basic curriculum subjects plus many enrichment
areas. For more Good Year Books, contact your local bookseller or
educational dealer. For a complete catalog with information about
other Good Year Books, please write:

Good Year Books
299 Jefferson Road
Parsippany, NJ 07054

Book Design: Meyers Design, Inc.
Editor: Laura Strom
Editorial Manager: Suzanne Beason
Executive Editor: Judy Adams
Copyright © 2000 Good Year Books, an imprint of Pearson Learning

ISBN 0-673-58662-6

1 2 3 4 5 6 7 8 9 - ML - 06 05 04 03 02 01 00 99

Acknowledgments

Our applause to Laura Strom and Roberta Dempsey, **who share our** sense of the importance of language.

Dedication

We dedicate this book to our students, who have **made teaching a joy.**

"Perhaps of all the creations of man, language is **the most astonishing.**"
Words and Poetry

Introduction

Introduction

The purpose of *The Grammar Handbook* is to provide you, the student, with a convenient grammar reference when you need to review the elements of language structure. Certain concepts will be new for some of you; therefore, this handbook will guide your understanding. For others, this book will serve as a refresher course and will aid the fine-tuning of your skills. Using this book will help you develop confidence in your writing ability.

The book begins with a grammar pre-test to encourage you to self-check your skill level and to identify those concepts on which you should focus your study. Each unit includes review sections with examples and simple exercises to test your knowledge of each unit. We suggest that you read the review sections, complete any practice exercises, and check the Answer Key. If you find you have missed a point, double-check the review section again. If necessary, you can clarify an issue with your English teacher. The book ends with a grammar post-test, which you can use to self-check your mastery of the concepts reviewed in this book.

Advantages of this book
- Independent study
- Condensed information for quick reference
- Practice exercises
- Pre-Tests and Post-Tests to self-check mastery of concepts
- Answer Key

The more you understand the grammar patterns of the English language, the more effectively you will write and speak. Excellent communication skills will give you both personal pleasure and academic rewards. In addition, those skills will serve you well in any field or job you choose in the future.

Pre-Test

1. Underline all nouns.
   - a. Every student in our class has gone on a field trip.
   - b. Carmen Lopez is the teacher in charge.
   - c. Only one large orange bus was used.
   - d. It actually had seat belts for each person.

2. Underline the subject nouns.
   - a. On the highway, the students saw four horses without riders.
   - b. Ms. Jensen's cell phone was used to call the police.
   - c. Manes flying and feet pounding, the horses ran very fast.
   - d. Beyond everyone's range of vision lay a barricade.
   - e. The barricade stopped the bus, the police, and the horses!

3. Underline all pronouns.
   - a. Have you been to the Field Museum with your friends?
   - b. It is a fascinating place for anyone to visit.
   - c. My cousins came to see us during the holidays, and they went to the Field Museum and the Adler Planetarium.
   - d. We wanted our families to go to the Art Institute to see the exhibit of Monet's paintings.
   - e. I myself will conduct a tour for them.

4. Underline all verbs.
   - a. After we flew to Florida last summer, we went with friends to the beach in Clearwater.
   - b. We had fun as we searched for shells in the sand near our condo.
   - c. Have you had that experience?
   - d. All of us waded and swam for hours every day.

    e. Beth's little sister shrieked with pleasure when waves washed over her.

    f. We will show you our pictures next week.

5. Underline all adjectives.

    a. The brilliant sunset was absolutely beautiful.

    b. Violet, pink, and gray hues colored the sky.

    c. Bright streaks of color crisscrossed on the dark horizon.

    d. In the eastern sky moved soft white clouds.

    e. The lovely end of the day was truly welcome.

6. Underline all adverbs.

    a. The hike we planned was a very difficult one.

    b. We could not finish it easily; everyone was too tired.

    c. At the top of the trail was an outstandingly beautiful view.

    d. The next day we walked slowly and carefully along the narrow edge.

    e. Soon we were seeing a truly astounding panorama.

    f. Cautiously we climbed down hoping not to slip on the dangerously sharp rocks.

7. Underline all prepositions and prepositional phrases.

    a. In the park could be seen several groups of children who were a safe distance from the parking lot.

    b. Some boys and girls sat under the oak trees working with craft kits.

    c. Four girls were playing tennis on the clay courts between the park buildings.

    d. Flying overhead, a huge dragon kite was held by two small boys in white shirts and blue shorts.

    e. Beside the flower beds planted underneath the bird statue, young mothers watched their babies crawling on the grass.

8. Underline all conjunctions.
    a. Should we plan the picnic now, or should we wait until tomorrow?
    b. Josh would help, but he has to work all weekend.
    c. Both Ann and Len will be available for food shopping, and Ray will drive them to the store.
    d. However, we need more volunteers for such a large outing, and we're sure we will find them.
    e. Since we have three weeks for preparation, we can either start our lists now or wait until Saturday.
    f. No one wants to wait; therefore, let's get busy and phone for those volunteers.

9. Underline all interjections.
    a. Oh no! The Bulls are losing this game.
    b. Watch that Michael Jordan!
    c. Would you—please!—help me get tickets.
    d. Now—look at that tricky play!

10. Underline all phrases.
    a. Eighth graders at the Wilson Elementary School are planning a trip to Washington, D.C., in May.
    b. Helping with the details are three teachers.
    c. Checking into a small hotel will be the first step on arrival in the city at six o'clock.
    d. The next day they intend to begin their tour of the city.
    e. They will enjoy views of the Lincoln and Jefferson Memorials and the Vietnam Wall.
    f. To visit Congress will also be exciting for the students from Wilson.

11. Indicate **Ph**rase or **Cl**ause at the right.
    a. in a dream of FantasyLand _____
    b. under a tree could be seen a four-eared deer _____
    c. squirrels with purple ears and tails _____
    d. a green monkey, swinging on a silver branch _____
    e. four parrots sang several songs in Spanish _____
    f. red-eyed horses, smaller than kittens _____

12. Identify the following clauses as **I**ndependent or **D**ependent.
    a. which is the way to study, of course   _____
    b. you could offer to help the students   _____
    c. if the teachers consider that a possibility   _____
    d. be sure to check their decision   _____

13. Identify the verbs in the following sentences as **Tr**ansitive, **Intr**ansitive, or **L**inking.
    a. All the children are excited about our trip.   _____
    b. Yes, we will leave Tuesday morning.   _____
    c. We have been planning for many weeks.   _____
    d. Brandon has been an excellent helper.   _____
    e. Please pack the supplies in that green box.   _____
    f. Could you help us, Meg?   _____

14. Correct any shifts in tense or voice of the verb.
    a. Bob will go to night school and would take a course in accounting.
    b. He wants a degree, and the degree will be appreciated.

15. Identify the verbals in each sentence as **G**erund, **P**articiple, or **Inf**initive.
    a. The children have had an exciting time at the amusement park.   _____
    b. Running from one place to another was part of their fun.   _____
    c. Ralph couldn't decide what to do first.   _____
    d. His twin, Rebecca, liked riding the airplanes.   _____
    e. The entire group wanted to have as much fun as possible.   _____
    f. They also enjoyed the tantalizing odors of popcorn and hot dogs.   _____

16. Underline the subject with one line and the verb with two lines.
     a.   Under the porch of the old house lived two rabbits and one small chipmunk.
     b.   That unusual trio played together quite happily.

Underline the direct object.
     a.   You may want their assistance with the break-in.
     b.   Could he have been the thief in the apartment?

Underline the indirect object.
     a.   Yes, he bought the flowers for his grandmother.
     b.   He also gave her a silver watch.

Underline the predicate noun or the predicate adjective.
     a.   From what they say, his manner is confident.
     b.   Consequently, Porter has been a good Congressman.

17. Correct any misplaced or dangling modifiers in the following sentences.
     a.   Lucy found the lost bracelet crawling over the sand dunes.
     b.   When only six years old, Lucy's mother bought their cottage on the lakefront.
     c.   To run in the marathon at the lake, discipline and effort are critical.
     d.   Hanging low on Lucy's waist, he saw a belt made of silver buckles.
     e.   When in a canoe alone, caution and alertness must be observed.

18. Identify the following sentences as **S**imple, **C**ompound, **C**omple**x** (**CX**), or **C**ompound-**C**omplex (**CC**).
     a.   People were not surprised when the blizzard came.   _____
     b.   Were you driving on the highway?   _____
     c.   We heard on the news that the airport was swarming with people.   _____
     d.   Many cars were stranded in the snow, but our family drove home safely.   _____
     e.   Some cars, buried beneath twenty inches of snow, were not uncovered for three days.   _____

f. Any vehicle that had a four-wheel drive
    could handle the snow drifts better than
    other cars; consequently, those were
    highly satisfactory that night.   _____

19. Identify the following sentences as **A**ctive or **P**assive construction.
    a. The drama group has been given a special
        grant.   _____
    b. Five appearances will be offered this spring. _____
    c. Les and Marna will be the leads in every
        play.   _____
    d. Marna is an extremely talented actress. _____
    e. She was awarded a prized trophy last June. _____
    f. Les will probably win one this year.   _____

20. Correct any non-parallel sentence elements.
    a. Bob is learning how to study, the way to organize
        his time, and how to concentrate.
    b. After school is out, Bob and his father can go fishing,
        sailing, or take a hike on rugged trails.

21. Correct any faulty coordination or subordination.
    a. She will resign from the cast of the play, and she
        will do so at the end of the week.
    b. The other actors were disappointed when they
        heard of her resignation.

22. Identify all sentence errors as **F**ragment, **R**un-**O**n (**RO**), or
    Comma **S**plice (**CS**).
    a. Running away from the school bus
        yesterday.   _____
    b. We could see Jeff but we couldn't spot Jose. _____
    c. In order to keep everyone on schedule.   _____
    d. Finally, the bus was on its way again, the
        children shouted happily.   _____
    e. They reached school on time, however
        it was a close call.   _____
    f. Roberto, a truly fine driver for the
        transportation company.   _____

23. Punctuate the following sentences.
    a. Our friends are a lot alike but they have very different hobbies.
    b. Grace Edna and Joyce enjoy collecting china animals.
    c. They collect cats dogs and birds however they are now considering looking for cow and pig figurines.
    d. Jesse and Brent have one hobby sports.
    e. Sachiko told Kim Painting is what I like to do.
    f. Could you listen quiet please to this announcement.

24.
    a. Define a topic sentence.
    b. Define a thesis statement.

UNIT 1

Nouns

REVIEW
The **noun** is one of the most important parts of speech. A noun names persons, places, things, animals, ideas, and actions. (A thing can be either tangible or intangible.) Nouns have two categories: common and proper. Proper nouns—the names of people, countries, languages, companies, and so on—are capitalized.

Common Nouns	Proper Nouns
animal	French
child	Sam
idea	England
city	Dallas
course	Marie

PRACTICE A. Underline all nouns in the following sentences.

1. Justice and truth are keystones in our concept of law in the United States.
2. Betsy and Bert spoke at length about their trip to Belgium last fall.
3. Many ideas have been advanced by archaeologists to explain the exodus of certain tribes from the high plains.
4. Both men and women enjoy an energetic game of tennis.
5. Jenna's final song was a "thing of beauty and a joy forever."
6. Four recipes in the new cookbook used rice and sauce to create delicious casseroles of unusual quality.
7. The matinee was a happy event for all the children and adults.

PRACTICE B. Fill in the blanks with nouns.

    1. Could _____ take the _____ to the library?

    2. _____ ate all the _____ I baked yesterday.

    3. Lana writes _____ and _____ for magazines.

    4. The _____ took _____, _____, and _____ to the beach.

PRACTICE C. Underline all nouns.

    1. Bob worked in the garden for hours, cultivating the tomatoes, squash, and beans.

    2. Around the corner came a huge caravan of campers, all sizes and all kinds.

    3. Starting from the company parking lot, some of the people had traveled for hours.

    4. Their plans included a picnic for about 200 people and a musical show on Saturday.

    5. The campers were a mixed group: children, students, women, businessmen—even a few cowboys.

    6. When Rod saw the parade of people, he left his work and joined the happy vacationers.

    7. For that day and the following one, relaxation and fun were highlights for everyone in the crowd.

UNIT 2
Subject Nouns

REVIEW   **Nouns** are used frequently and appear in special positions in sentences. One vital use of a noun is as the
subject of a sentence or, in other words, as the director
of the action or situation. Most often, the subject nouns
will be placed at or near the beginning of a sentence.

> *Chicago* is one of the largest cities in the United States.
> The hungry *baby* drank his milk quickly.

Note: When the subject follows the verb and appears toward
or at the end of a sentence, the sentence becomes an
example of inversion.

> Under the chair lay her *cat.*
> Behind her stood her best *friend.*

REVIEW   Sentences may have **compound subjects** (more than
one subject noun).

> Exhausted, *Jon* and *Bill* collapsed on the lawn.
> *Greg, Mark,* and *Todd* ushered at the concert.
> Beyond the line of trees could be seen one *moon,*
> two *stars,* and three *planes.*

PRACTICE A. Underline the subject nouns.
1. On the river, the excursion boat moved majestically toward us.
2. Our new car has performed well on the highway.
3. In a small velvet box lay an expensive ring.
4. The three tall players come from Chile.
5. Lesley and Raymond have built a racing car.
6. Regardless of the attention last week, the local newspaper has not retracted its statement.
7. Under the gloves and scarves can be found the envelope with the money.

PRACTICE B. Fill in the blanks with subject nouns.
1. _____ and _____ walked to the store to buy milk.
2. Thin and frail, the _____ approached them.
3. To my right paraded the _____.
4. As soon as possible, _____, _____, and _____ will remove their books.

PRACTICE C. Underline the subject nouns.
1. Dogs and cats can live happily together in the same house.
2. Matter of fact, one cat of Fran's raised a puppy.
3. That puppy acted more like a cat than a dog.
4. Under the puppy's soft black fur, however, beat the heart of a small lion.
5. The two animals, side by side, greeted all the guests at the front door.
6. Meowing and barking, Mutt and Jeff amused the visitors and sometimes annoyed them as well.
7. In order to get more attention from the guests, the cat would leap off the upper landing into the middle of the room.

UNIT 3
Verbs

REVIEW   **Verbs** are action words; they also express a state of being.

> At the zoo, the lions *roar*.
> Chelle *visited* her grandmother yesterday.
> Julius *is* an excellent student.
> The situation *became* alarming.

Sentences can have compound verbs (two or more verbs).

> Jerry *clapped* and *clapped* for the clowns.
> Our children *ran* and *played* all afternoon.

REVIEW   Verbs can be identified as **regular** or **irregular**.

Regular verbs follow a consistent pattern to change from present tense to past tense to the past participle.

Irregular verbs do not follow a pattern but change form.

Some examples are noted below.

	Verb	**Past Tense**	**Past Participle**
Regular	walk	walked	walked
	follow	followed	followed
Irregular	be	was	been
	go	went	gone
	lead	led	led
	lie	lay	lain
	run	ran	run
	teach	taught	taught

A few verbs do not change forms.

	Verb	**Past Tense**	**Past Participle**
Invariables	burst	burst	burst
	hit	hit	hit

Note: Check a dictionary to answer questions about the principal parts of any verb.

REVIEW **Auxiliary** (helping) **verbs** are used with other verbs to show tense, mood, or voice.

be	have	ought
can	may	shall
could	might	should
do	must	will
has	need	would

The balloon of water has burst and hit my uncle's head.
The papers have lain there for several days.

                       (past tense) (present tense)

Incorrect When Janna *walked* home, she *sees* an old friend.

                       (past tense)   (past tense)

Correct When Janna *walked* home, she *saw* an old friend.

                            (present tense)

Incorrect When the temperature rises to an almost
                               (past tense)
unbearable degree, we stayed inside.

                            (present tense)

Correct When the temperature rises to an almost
                             (present tense)
unbearable degree, we stay inside.

REVIEW   The **voice** of a verb can be active or passive. Active voice is identified in sentences with subjects that act. Passive voice is identified in sentences in which the subject is acted upon.

> **Active voice:**   Hemingway wrote many books.
> **Passive voice:**   Many books were written by Hemingway.

Note: Only transitive verbs can change their voice because only such verbs have direct objects. (For further clarification, see Unit 10.)

Whenever possible, use the active voice of the verbs to give a crisp, dynamic effect. Although a weak construction, the passive voice can be used to vary the voice deliberately, to set an impersonal tone, or to avoid placing blame. (For further clarification, see Unit 12.)

Caution!   Avoid shifting from active to passive voice in the same sentence. The shift creates an awkward construction.

> (active)
> **Incorrect**   After Larry *mowed* the lawn, an edger
> (passive)
> *was used* along the sidewalk.

> (active)   (active)
> **Correct**   After Larry *mowed* the lawn, he *used* an edger along the sidewalk.

> (active)
> **Incorrect**   Leila *arranged* the flowers, and then
> (passive)
> the table *was set*.

> (active)
> **Correct**   Leila *arranged* the flowers, and then
> (active)
> she *set* the table.

PRACTICE A. Underline all verbs.

1. A cold north wind howled around the eaves and whistled down the chimney.
2. What can they do about the locusts? What have they tried to do in other years?
3. Their friends hoped to persuade the authorities to grant them a license for the new club.
4. His word is good enough for the judge, a strict man at times.
5. Each season seems off-balance this year. Are we wrong to think so?
6. The world is ready to consider peace, but what are the prospects?
7. Carolers were humming and singing in the corridors of the nursing home.

PRACTICE B. Fill in the blanks with verbs.

1. He _____ at the man who took his wallet.
2. Some people _____ and _____ at the cafe.
3. For example, that family _____ or _____ or _____.
4. Even though he _____ the red light, he _____ the car in the intersection.

PRACTICE C. Underline all verbs.

1. The families on the beach enjoyed the entire day away from the heat of the city.
2. Children jumped and played in the sand and built magnificent sand castles.
3. They were happy and felt relaxed for the first time in months.
4. Their parents stretched out in the warm sunshine and yawned lazily.
5. For the rest of the day, they had nothing to do.
6. Can you imagine their pleasure on those golden beaches?
7. Within the shade of the large umbrella rested many vacationers.

PRACTICE D. Identify shifts of tense or voice and the verb involved.

1. When Janna comes here, she always asked for popcorn. _____
2. As they packed their books, they write down the titles. _____
3. Many boxes of popcorn were eaten in the past, and she also eats candy. _____
4. Although Stephen likes swimming, bowling has also been enjoyed by him. _____

PRACTICE E. In the blanks at the right, identify any shift of tense or voice and the verbs involved.

1. When the wind blew down the door, Sam is afraid.   _____

2. The storm was predicted, but it was more severe than expected.   _____

3. Our children inside were safe; however, their children had been left outside.   _____

4. Some families listen to warnings; some obviously did not.   _____

UNIT 4
Pronouns

REVIEW **Pronouns** substitute for nouns and are divided into several categories. One group contains personal pronouns that replace nouns used to name people, animals, and so on. The pattern below identifies these important personal pronouns and their usage.

Singular	Subjective Case*	Objective Case**	Possessive Case***	
1st person	I	me	my	mine
2nd person	you	you	your	yours
3rd person	he	him	his	his
	she	her	her	hers
	it	it	its	its
Plural				
1st person	we	us	ours	ours
2nd person	you	you	your	yours
3rd person	they	them	their	theirs
Special	who	whom	whose	

*   Words are used as subject words or in the predicate noun position.

**   These words are used as direct objects or object of prepositions (and some as indirect objects).

***These words are used as adjectives.

1st person—Singular—Subjective *I* eat yogurt everyday.
3rd person—Plural—Objective Our team elected *them*.
Special—Subjective Lee is the man *who* will represent us.
Special—Objective Hester is the one *whom* you met
yesterday.
Special—Possessive *Whose* is that?

Pronouns in another category act as **reflexives** or **intensifiers**. A reflexive pronoun refers to the subject noun or pronoun of a sentence.

> Father is blaming *himself.*
> They seem to have deceived *themselves.*
> Johnny threw *himself* on the sofa.

The intensifier, as its name suggests, reinforces a noun or pronoun.

> Joan *herself* will sew the costumes.
> They *themselves* realize the error.

A third category contains **indefinite pronouns** that are used in place of nouns, or often, with nouns.

all	everyone	none
another	few	one
anybody	many	other
both	much	some
each	neither	
either	nobody	

> *Both* boys are funny; *each* is also intelligent.
> We bought food at the Chinese restaurant; *some* of it was a new taste for us but delicious.

Relative pronouns show a relationship to another word or idea. A few of these pronouns are found in other categories as well.

that	which	whom
what	who	whose

> Angelo ate the steak, *which* was all right with Dad.
> My grandparents like books *that* are historical novels.

The fifth category includes the few **demonstrative pronouns**.

Singular	**Plural**
this	these
that	those

This hat belongs to the coach.

These flowers belong to *that* woman.

The last group of pronouns includes both the cardinal numbers (one, two, three, four, five, and so on) and the ordinal numbers (first, second, third, fourth, fifth, and so on).

Louise bought *four* souvenirs, but Lisa bought only *two* items.

The *second* cake looks beautiful, but the *fourth* one tastes the best.

Note: The noun to which a pronoun refers is called the *antecedent*. Place the pronoun as close as possible to that noun to be sure the reference is clear. Furthermore, pronouns must agree with the nouns they replace. If a pronoun replaces a singular noun, the pronoun must also be singular; if the noun is plural, the pronoun must also be plural. Use pronouns in the subjective case to replace nouns in subject positions. Use pronouns in the objective case to replace nouns in object positions.

John ate the meat; he liked it.

Singular   *He* refers to *John*. (subjective case)
Pronouns   *It* refers to *meat*. (objective case)

John and *meat* are the antecedents for *he* and *it*.

Our classmates chose Mary and Grace; they truly liked them.

Plurals   *They* refers to *classmates.* (subjective case)
Them refers to *Mary and Grace.* (objective case)

Classmates and *Mary and Grace* are the antecedents for *they* and *them*.

PRACTICE A. Underline all pronouns.
1. They have eaten the cake today, but we can have some tomorrow.
2. Our members won blue ribbons; all were delighted.
3. Lisa purchased apartments in that building; she puts her money into real-estate ventures.
4. Dad mailed the package to us, but we sent it to the person who ordered the merchandise last month.
5. This contest is a good one for you; your poetry should win first or second prize.
6. Anyone can try for that position; someone has to earn it.
7. Those children wanted only pennies from him, but they received several dollars.

PRACTICE B. Fill in the blanks with appropriate pronouns.
1. The president _____ ordered the _____ men to bring _____ weapons to the armory.
2. _____ can join _____ group.
3. Bill wants _____ books; _____ needs _____ for his new courses.
4. You will need _____ pairs of shoes and _____ heavy sweater for _____ cool days.

PRACTICE C. Underline all pronouns.

1. Anyone can see the driver is having trouble with her car.
2. In the first place, three vehicles in line behind her were honking loudly; others pushed too close to the car in front.
3. We went over to the driver and asked if she could use our help.
4. It was rather obvious to us: She needed assistance with the two children who were screaming at the tops of their voices.
5. Those children were shouting, "I want my Mommy! I want my Mommy!"
6. Everyone standing there offered either to get a mechanic, whose skills would benefit the car, or a nurse, who could quiet the frightened children, which would have been most welcome.
7. Your guess is as good as mine as to which offer she took.

UNIT 5
Adjectives

REVIEW   **Adjectives** are words that modify nouns; that is, they are words that add information about nouns. Adjectives most often describe or limit nouns.

Descriptive Adjectives	**Limiting Adjectives**
green grass	*some* crackers
robin-blue eggs	*her* book
smooth skin	*second* room

Note: Limiting adjectives are often pronouns.
Proper adjectives are formed from nouns.

five books	*her* hat
that car	*your* choice
Mother's Day	*New Jersey's* coast
Jean's coat	*Texas* sun

Adjectivals are nouns, or sometimes phrases and clauses, that appear in the adjective positions but are not regular adjectives.

afternoon matinee	heart *of gold*
pledge *of faith*	*twilight* walk
tone *that was dripping with venom*	

Some adjectives show comparison. Comparative and superlative degrees may be developed from the basic word (the positive degree) in one of three ways.

1. Use *-er* and *-est* with the positive degree:

Positive	**Comparative**	**Superlative**
happy	happier	happiest

2. Use *more* and *most* to form a short phrase:

Positive	Comparative	Superlative
reverent	*more* reverent	*most* reverent
thoughtful	*more* thoughtful	*most* thoughtful

3. Use irregular forms:

Positive	Comparative	Superlative
good	better	best
bad	worse	worst

Note: Use the comparative degree, *-er* and *more*, to show similarities between two persons or actions; use the superlative degree, *-est* and *most*, when comparing more than two. *Never combine the two degrees*.

Note: Not only regular adjectives, nouns, or pronouns but also verbals (not verbs) act as adjectives. (For further clarification on verbals, see Unit 13.)

The *exciting* films won our praise.
Her *aged* parents were warm, friendly people.
The gymnastic events were *thrilling*.
The *swollen* river ran over its banks.

Adjectives are sometimes used as nouns.

The *pink* in your dress is a distinctive touch.
Neat is the way I want it.

PRACTICE A. Underline all adjectives.

1. Large houses have great appeal for families with many children.
2. Those foolish children ate all the black and the purple jelly beans before dinner.
3. That violent storm cut a wide swath through the center of the old part of town.
4. Colored balloons, red, green, yellow, and blue, were part of the young acrobat's act.
5. Her charming manner is only one of her basic appeals to her audience.
6. Sweet and soft, the music of Bach rose high above our heads.
7. She has the most beautiful eyes of all the young contestants.

PRACTICE B. Fill in the blanks with adjectives.

1. _____ _____ horses ran around the _____ field.
2. When Jim eats pizza, he has a _____ smile on his _____ face.
3. A _____ _____ day makes Becky feel _____.
4. Those books, _____ and _____, are quite valuable.

PRACTICE C. Underline all adjectives.

1. The happy bride accepted good wishes from her family and old friends.
2. The long line made an impressive sight for those guests who arrived late.
3. The young bridesmaids wore lavender chiffon gowns and lavender satin sandals.
4. Bright bouquets of spring flowers were tied with lavender and purple ribbons.
5. Wooden tables had been set up to hold huge silver trays of delicious hors d'oeuvres.
6. Bob, the groom, tall and handsome, had a slightly dazed look on his face.
7. That look was matched by the expression, pale and frazzled, on his new father-in-law's face.

UNIT 6
Adverbs

REVIEW An **adverb** modifies a verb, an adjective, or another adverb.

Adverbs answer these important questions:
How?	Why?
Where?	How much?
When?	To what degree?

Many adverbs end with -*ly*, but not all.
perfectly	quite	not
clearly	very	
really	well	

Many adverbs show comparison by the use of *more* or *most*.
rapidly
more rapidly
most rapidly

Prepositions and nouns are frequently used as adverbs.

Preposition He is moving *forward*.
Noun My sister broke her leg *today*.

Caution! Do not confuse adverbs with adjectives.

Incorrect Jack's skiff handles easier than Jim's.
Correct Jack's skiff handles more *easily* than Jim's.
Incorrect The movie is real stimulating.
Correct The movie is *really* stimulating.

One traffic idiom uses the phrase *Drive Slow*.

PRACTICE A. Underline all adverbs.
1. This morning she swam quickly to help the child who was screaming loudly.
2. The phone rang so often today that her head throbs painfully.
3. Our friends will arrive soon; it is almost time for their train.
4. Write immediately for directions; however, if the response is too slow, come get a copy from us.
5. That speech sounds really pompous, but perhaps we're too critical.
6. All commuter trains are running slowly this afternoon, so do not plan on arriving early.
7. He can row more quickly and easily than Bob.

PRACTICE B. Fill in the blanks with adverbs.
1. Roberto is the _____ musical of the four brothers.
2. You were _____ kind _____.
3. The boat moves, _____ and _____, down the river.
4. He plays tennis _____ _____.

PRACTICE C. Underline all adverbs.
1. The condition of the classroom was quite chaotic.
2. The leaders of the student body were too outraged about the daringly bold raid of the rival football team to be sensible.
3. That morning they had found a deep hole in the middle of the playing field; in that very deep hole had been planted a very tall tree.
4. Silently and slowly, the principal walked into the now quiet room.
5. Mr. Brayton was really angry, but he was thoroughly in control of himself.
6. He spoke softly that morning to the truly repentant students and suggested firmly that they settle down.
7. Now the solution seemed somewhat obvious—clearly obvious.

UNIT 7
Prepositions

REVIEW   A **preposition** is a connecting word in a sentence. There are two kinds of prepositions: simple and compound.

Simple		Compound
about	despite	according to
above	except	across from
against	for	because of
before	inside	except for
beneath	over	in addition to
by	until	on account of

Most prepositions head a phrase (a unit of related words) that ends with a noun or a pronoun.

around it	*for* Ben	*under* his head
behind him	*to* the zoo	*except for* Harry

Prepositions can also be used as clause markers and thus become subordinating conjunctions (see Unit 8).

We will stay at the club *until* you come back.
Before the day is over, you will receive an exciting surprise.

Note: Contemporary usage permits a preposition to appear at the end of a sentence, particularly at the end of a question (especially in informal speech).

What are you looking *for?*
What are you talking *about?*

Caution!   Do not repeat the same preposition in a sentence.

Incorrect	Do you have the book to which he was referring to?
Correct	Do you have the book to which he was referring?

Incorrect	This is the subject of which I was speaking of.
Correct	This is the subject of which I was speaking.

Drop the second preposition in each sentence. Note that sentences using a preposition and the word *which* frequently double the preposition incorrectly.

Caution!   Be careful to distinguish between prepositional phrases and infinitives. The preposition *to* with the root of a verb forms an infinitive. Note again that the prepositional phrase ends with a noun or a pronoun (objective case) as the object of the preposition. (For further clarification of infinitives, see Unit 13.)

Prepositional Phrase	**Infinitives**
to the village	to dance
to her house	to jump
to his car	to consider

PRACTICE A. Underline all prepositions and prepositional phrases.

1. The socks can be found in the drawer on the right-hand side.
2. What type of house are you interested in?
3. Underneath the tree lay a white cat with five kittens.
4. Her dress of silk was an outstanding entry in the fashion show that we went to see last night.
5. We need a bottle of milk, five pounds of sugar, and a pound of coffee.
6. Whatever you are looking for is not to be found below the window.
7. When Jason sat down next to Daphne, he lost the wallet that had been tucked in his back pocket.

PRACTICE B. Fill in the blanks with prepositions.
1. Look _____ that book _____
   the second shelf.
2. You might look _____ the Degas painting
   _____ the next room.
3. Her sweater, made _____ England, is
   _____ fine wool.
4. _____ the horizon lies a dream world
   _____ blue skies.

PRACTICE C. Underline all prepositions and prepositional phrases.
1. Under the table can be found a child of five, a small
   package of mischief.
2. His pranks during the day cause consternation within
   the family.
3. Under the circumstances, his father must be told
   about his naughty son.
4. His father, who has been working at a company
   with its headquarters in a northern province of
   Canada, will be disturbed to hear the news.
5. Outside his interest in work, Jake Dolen's only other
   concern is for his child.
6. He hides his feelings beneath a somewhat gruff
   exterior and keeps his thoughts to himself.
7. His car should be coming into the driveway about
   8:00, and he will walk through the door by 8:10.

UNIT 8
Conjunctions

REVIEW   A **conjunction** is used as a connector in a sentence and shows a relationship among ideas. Conjunctions fall into four categories:

1. Coordinating

and	nor	
but	or	
(sometimes) for	so	yet

Coordinating conjunctions connect equal words, phrases, and clauses. As clause connectors, they are most often used in compound or compound-complex sentences.

> black *and* white
> to the store *and* to the church
> honest *but* tactful

The students are present, *and* one of them will be the moderator for the meeting.

True, he has limited experience, *but* he is definitely the best candidate.

2. Correlatives (pairs)

both – and
either – or
neither – nor
not only – but also
whether – or

The correlatives are closely related to the coordinating conjunctions. However, these connectors are different because they appear in pairs.

The arrangement is *not only* fair *but* is *also* generous.

You should *either* send Mr. Bownsall a telegram today *or* call him before noon tomorrow.

Note: The correlatives should be kept as close as possible to the words they join.

3. **Subordinating**	although	before	until
	as	if	when
	because	since	while

These conjunctions head dependent clauses at the beginning, middle, or end of a sentence. The list of subordinating conjunctions is long, so only a few are noted here.

If the time is right, you can act.
She cannot attend the meeting *because* it conflicts with her classes.

Note:

Other parts of speech, such as adverbs and prepositions, sometimes become subordinating conjunctions.

Before the day is over, you will meet the professor. (preposition as a conjunction)

Enter *when* your name is called. (adverb as a conjunction)

4. **Conjunctive Adverbs**	accordingly	moreover
	consequently	nevertheless
	however	therefore

Conjunctive adverbs usually connect independent clauses and may be used in various positions in sentences. Only a few are listed here.

Homer overslept; *consequently,* he was late for class.
He has worked hard; *therefore,* he deserves a vacation.

PRACTICE A. Underline all conjunctions.
1. You may go to the party, but we are going to study for the chemistry exam.
2. Do you want to study with us, or do you have to go to work?
3. The next lesson is difficult; however, I think we can understand it.
4. Since we started our work this morning, we have finished eight pages.
5. When the alarm clock rings, let me know.
6. We may stay in our study group until the sun comes up.
7. The lecture was both interesting and puzzling.

PRACTICE B. Fill in the blanks with conjunctions.
1. _____ it's late, we could go to the theater _____ have dinner afterward.
2. _____ Pepe _____ Jose is a good golfer, _____ they are superb tennis players.
3. You may try this recipe _____ that one.
4. He won't come _____ the shop is closed.

PRACTICE C. Underline all conjunctions.
1. Both newspaper and TV forecasts of the weather have been threatening, but we are not alarmed.
2. If the high winds become stronger, however, we should take shelter.
3. Although Aaron and Trish have taken the children to the basement, we have not asked our children to join them.
4. The last warning seemed serious; nevertheless, we will remain cautious and double-check the information.

5. Neither the telephone nor the radio is operating properly, so we must conclude the storm warnings are correct.
6. Since the others have gone, Brad and I should hurry to join them.
7. The storm was unusually violent; therefore, we'll pay more attention in the future to the weather forecasters.

UNIT 9
Interjections

REVIEW **Interjections** are expressions of feeling. This part of speech may be a sound that reflects varying degrees of emotions, or it may be a word, phrase, or sentence that conveys special meaning.

> Oh!
> Watch out!
> He broke my glasses!

Caution! Never overdo the exclamation. Too many interjections detract from a satisfactory style of writing.

PRACTICE A. Underline all interjections.
1. Be careful! That water is hot.
2. Ouch! I hit my knee on the door.
3. Please watch your step!
4. Move it here—no!—here.
5. Your poem is excellent!
6. Did you see that dive? Look!
7. You must be mistaken!

UNIT 10
Kinds of Verbs

REVIEW   Verbs are identified as **transitive**, **intransitive**, or **linking**.

Most transitive verbs (TV) are action verbs that require a direct object (DO) to complete the meaning of the sentence. Direct objects are nouns or pronouns that receive the effect of the action. They answer the questions of *what* or *whom*.

(TV)   (DO)
Three men *designed* the *building*.

(TV)   (DO)
Kyle *missed her.*

Note: Some transitive verbs do not indicate direct actions, but they do require a direct object.

(TV)   (DO)
Henry *received* an *award*.

(TV)   (DO)
Sara *owns* two fur *coats*.

An intransitive verb (IV) does not need a direct object to complete the meaning of the sentence; it can stand alone with its subject.

Mice *scamper.*   Four people *slipped* on the ice.
Dogs *bark.*   Can you *come* here?

Some verbs can be used either as transitive or as intransitive verbs.

(TV)   (DO)

The coach *shouted commands.*

(IV)

He *shouted* into a megaphone.

(TV)   (DO)

John *caught* the *ball.*

(IV)

His shirt *caught* on the fence.

A few verbs, such as *lie* (to recline) or *rise,* are always intransitive.

Grandmother *lies* down in the afternoon.

The students *lay* on the grass in the sun.

Smoke *rises* from the chimney.

PRACTICE A. Underline the verbs and identify them at the right as **Tr**ansitive or **Intr**ansitive
1. Our friends have just eaten dinner with their cousins.   _____
2. Can you reach that book for me?   _____
3. Martha will sing in the concert on Monday. _____
4. Lester wrote four books on the subject of trout fishing.   _____
5. The space shuttle rose rapidly into the sky. _____
6. Meg swims at the pool every day.   _____
7. Consider the case closed.   _____

REVIEW   Linking verbs (LV) connect the subject to the predicate noun (PN) that restates the subject, or to a predicate adjective (PA) that describes the subject. Linking verbs are the forms of the verb *be (is, are, am, was, were, been),* plus a special group of verbs, such as those following, that can also be linking verbs in certain constructions (some are sense verbs):

appear	feel	prove	smell
become	get	remain	stand
continue	grow	seem	taste
elect	look	sound	turn

      (LV)   (PN)
Robert *turned* traitor.

       (LV) (PA)
Constance *seemed* sad.

          (LV) (PN)
The groom's name *was* Joshua.

  (LV)(PA)
Dad *feels* ill.

        (LV)   (PN)
Bill Clinton *has remained* our president.

     (LV)(PA)
The moon *is* bright tonight.

     (LV)   (PN)
Craig *has been* the treasurer of the club.

    (LV) (PA)
Our friends *were* happy.

Caution!   The verb *be* can be used not only as a linking verb, but also combines with other verbs to become transitive or intransitive.

(TV)   (PN)
Marcia *has been* the recorder.

(LV) (PA)
Mrs. Brown *was* furious.

(TV)   (DO)
Vince *is buying* my horse.

(TV)   (DO)
They *are planning* a picnic.

(IV)
Her baby *is crying*.

(IV)
She *has been fussing* since two o'clock.

PRACTICE B. Underline the verbs and identify them as **Tr**ansitive or **L**inking.

1. Andre hit the ball into the grandstand yesterday.   _____
2. He is a good player at all times.   _____
3. Those individuals in the front row are senators.   _____
4. Patrick cooked our dinner over an open fire. _____
5. His skill is outstanding.   _____
6. Morrie's father bought a sports car.   _____
7. Lela seems quite unresponsive today.   _____

PRACTICE C. Identify each kind of verb (**T**, **I**, **L**) and any direct object, predicate noun, or predicate adjective (**DO**, **PN**, **PA**).

	Kind of Verb	DO, PN, or PA
1. When will they return?	_____	_____
2. Luciann is taking art history this semester.	_____	_____
3. That premise had been proved wrong.	_____	_____
4. Some fairy tales frighten children.	_____	_____
5. My favorite orchestra was here last week.	_____	_____
6. Jenny's mother is an executive at an insurance company.	_____	_____
7. The roses in our garden have never been more beautiful.	_____	_____

PRACTICE D. Underline the verbs and identify them as **Tr**ansitive, **I**ntransitive, or **L**inking.

1. Roger always orders lobster for his birthday. _____

2. His wife, a young Japanese woman, appears shy with Roger's old friends. _____

3. Their recent trip to Japan lasted four weeks. _____

4. Roger first met Yoshiko's family in Tokyo. _____

5. Succumbing to Roger's charm, the grandmother bought him a handsome, complicated camera. _____

6. They were excited about the special trip. _____

7. At home again after their trip, they are resting. _____

UNIT 11
Indirect Objects and Objective Complements

REVIEW   In other units, the sentence elements of the predicate verb, direct object, predicate noun, and predicate adjective have been reviewed.

The **indirect object**, a noun or a pronoun, appears only with a small group of transitive verbs:

ask	find	make
build	give	offer
buy	hand	send

Usually, the indirect object (IO) precedes the direct object (DO); the prepositions *to* and *for* (sometimes *of*), which could be used before the indirect object, are understood.

(IO)   (DO)
Darrin sent *Kawanda* a birthday *present.*

(IO) (DO)
Dad handed *him* the *shovel.*

Sometimes, however, the indirect object is placed in a prepositional phrase and follows the direct object.

(DO)   (IO)
The teacher gave the *assignment* to *them.*

(DO) (IO)
Kerry took *flowers* to *her.*

A sentence cannot have an indirect object without a direct object.

PRACTICE A. Identify the direct object in Sentence **a** and the indirect object in Sentence **b**.

1. a. Father wrote a check for her tuition.
    b. Father wrote her a check for her tuition.
2. a. Mrs. Gray taught three basic dance steps.
    b. Mrs. Gray taught three basic dance steps to them.
3. a. Simon bought an algebra book.
    b. Simon bought Dick an algebra book.
4. a. Please throw that ball lying on the desk.
    b. Please throw Ginny that ball lying on the desk.
5. a. Melissa offered a ride to the library.
    b. Melissa offered me a ride to the library.
6. a. Bebe threw the Frisbee.
    b. Bebe threw the Frisbee to Diane.
7. a. Her uncle gave the news.
    b. Her uncle gave us the news.

PRACTICE B. Underline the indirect object.

1. Our professor returned our paper to us.
2. Our class sent her a sympathy note.
3. The students will prepare dinner for us.
4. Could you find the boxes for Aunt Lorena?
5. Susanne offered Ruth an opportunity to visit her family.
6. The principal assigned her a classroom.
7. Please build a bookcase for Mike.

REVIEW The **objective complement** is a word or phrase used to complete the meaning of the direct object. Only a small group of verbs can be used to create the objective complement.

appoint	declare	nominate
believe	fancy	prove
choose	make	suppose

The squad elected Kristen *head majorette.*
Dr. Madison appointed Martin *treasurer.*
Women think Paul Newman *handsome.*

Usually, the objective complement is a noun or an adjective, but pronouns, adverbs, and both present and past participles of verbs may be used.

Pronoun   Wes thought the leader *her.*

Adverb of place   We found her *upstairs.*

Verb, Present Participle   Zachary imagined her *sailing.*

Verb, Past Participle   His brother considered Alex *finished.*

Note: *To be* is implied before the objective complement.

PRACTICE C. Underline each direct object with one line and each objective complement with two lines.
1. Freshmen at Duke University elected Samuel class treasurer.
2. Mother found Tom Selleck fascinating.
3. Oh! I thought you upstairs.
4. We imagined him King of the Realm!
5. The doctor declared him recovered.
6. Lacey found the baby crying.
7. He fancied himself honest.

PRACTICE D. Underline the objective complement.
1. Belinda thought the argument convincing.
2. The committee designated Jack chairman.
3. I believed you cooperative.
4. Mr. Black found the dog outside.
5. Will you keep her smiling?
6. The voters nominated Warren village president.
7. Jackson called the actress exciting.

UNIT 12

Voice of the Verb—Active/Passive

REVIEW   Sentences with subjects that act contain **active verbs**. When the subject is acted upon, the sentence uses a **passive verb**.

> **Active Verb**   The batter *hit* a home run.

> **Passive Verb**   A home run *was hit* by the batter.

To change the voice of a verb from active to passive:

1. Make the direct object (DO) of the verb (V) the subject (S) of the new sentence.

2. Place the subject of the active verb in a *by* phrase or omit it from the new sentence.

3. Use the past participle (PP) of the verb with an appropriate form of the infinitive *to be*.

>   (S)   (V)   (DO)
> **Active Voice**   Three girls *sang* three songs.

>   (former DO)(to be)(PP)   (former S)
> **Passive Voice**   Three songs *were sung* by three girls.
>   or
>   Three songs *were sung*.
>   (the *by* phrase is omitted.)

To change the voice from passive to active:
1. Take the object of the preposition in the *by* phrase or create an actor, if there is no such phrase, for the subject.
2. Transfer the subject of the passive-voice sentence to the direct-object position.
3. Convert the past participle of the verb back to the appropriate tense of the verb and drop the form of the infinitive *to be*.

Passive Voice	The house *was sold* by Josephine.
Active Voice	Josephine *sold* the house.
	or
Passive Voice	The house *was sold.*
Active Voice	The new sales associate *sold* the house.

Note: Only transitive verbs can change their voice because only those verbs have direct objects.

Whenever possible, writers should use the active voice of the verb. However, the passive voice is useful when a writer:
a. wishes to set an impersonal tone;
b. does not know the "actor";
c. varies the use of voice;
d. does not wish to place blame.

PRACTICE A. Identify the following sentences as **A**ctive or **P**assive voice.
1. Pancakes and sausages will be served before the game.   _____
2. Mr. Grant, we have sent the tickets.   _____
3. Most people enjoy a really exciting baseball game.   _____
4. All the players have been given a new contract.   _____
5. Season tickets are being offered to the public.   _____
6. Until the first of the month, you may purchase tickets at a 10 percent discount.   _____
7. Long lines will be seen in front of the box offices.   _____

PRACTICE B. Rewrite the following sentences, changing from active voice to passive voice.

1. We will have a picnic in the park today.

   _____

2. Suzanne is baking a ham for sandwiches.

   _____

3. Les and Wes have planned a huge bonfire.

   _____

4. Usually we play many games.

   _____

Rewrite the following sentences, changing from passive voice to active voice.

5. Swimming will also be suggested.

   _____

6. After the games, dessert for everyone can be served.

   _____

7. Transportation for the entire group will be arranged.

   _____

8. Announcements for this special picnic have already been mailed.

   _____

PRACTICE C. Identify the following sentences as **A**ctive or **P**assive voice.

1. Our friends have taken interesting and profitable positions. _____

2. Two jobs in South America were rejected. _____

3. Karl accepted work on a ranch in South Dakota. _____

4. Last week a photographer's job was turned down. _____

5. An accounting firm had appeal for three friends. _____

6. Three sales positions at a large department store were not accepted. _____

7. We have written congratulations to all of them. _____

UNIT 13
Verbals

REVIEW The three verbals are the **infinitive**, the **gerund**, and the **participle**.

The infinitive consists of the preposition *to* plus the root of a verb. The preposition *to*, in this form, becomes "the sign of the infinitive."

to gamble	to jump
to make	to smile

Peg hoped *to become* a registered nurse.
Lester wants *to go* to New York City.

The gerund, an *-ing* form of a verb, is used as a noun in any of its functions: subject (S), object of the preposition (OP), the direct object (DO), or predicate noun (PN).

dancing	singing
smiling	swimming

(S)
Their excellent *singing* brought the audience to its feet.

(S)
Heavy *gambling* has been his downfall.

(DO)
She chose *dancing* as her major activity.

(PN)
Belden's hobby is *wrestling*.

(OP)
What should we give Beth for *trying?*

The participle, an *-ing, -ed,* or *-en* form of a verb, is used as an adjective.

cutting	delighted	fallen
rushing	frightened	given

Hope's *cutting* remarks hurt Mona.
The *delighted* child squealed with happiness.
Brooke is her *given* name.

Note: Not all *-ing* words are gerunds or participles. Combined with other verbs, *-ing* words can also be part of a predicate verb (main verb).

Verb Those students *are listening* to a taped lecture.

Gerund *Listening* was not easy for Sylvia, an eager talker.

Participle Her *listening* skills are excellent.

Verb Dad *has been cooking* dinner on the grill.

Gerund We cannot eat his *cooking* all the time.

Participle That *cooking* instructor came here last week.

Verb Renee *has been chosen* for the role of Juliet.

Gerund Have you seen *The Chosen,* an old movie?

Participle His *chosen* role in life puzzles me.

Note: Verbals will also appear in phrases.

to hear the truth	singing his praises
to run the risk	trying to win the award
listening at the door	dawdling on the way

Rhonda does not want *to hear the truth.*
Trying to win the award was her primary goal.
Listening at the door, Christopher was shocked by what he heard.

PRACTICE A. Underline all verbals.

1. Julio set a killing pace in the marathon last week.
2. To give up would be a discouraging example for Patrice.
3. Liam was whistling the other morning, but his whistling was quite off-key.
4. Twisting and turning, the river snaked its way through a canyon to join with the larger Colorado River.
5. In *The Scarlet Letter*, Hester was considered a fallen woman, and other women wanted little to do with her.
6. William's shouting angered his father, who wanted him to be quiet.
7. His peculiar behavior was frightening to Consuela, who didn't know how to react appropriately.

PRACTICE B. Underline the verbal phrases.

1. Cutting out sweets will help most people lose weight.
2. To be on time is hard for some students.
3. Maurice, thinking about his future, is hoping to become a lawyer.
4. "Running a tight ship" refers to a form of management.
5. Jumping up and down, Randy tried to hit the piñata.
6. Perhaps you should try to cut your prices.
7. Identifying your strengths and your weaknesses helps you to improve as a student.

PRACTICE C. From this list, choose verbs and insert them in the blanks in their appropriate forms. Try to use all the verbs.

perform   study   travel   ring   cope
sing   charm

1. They could hear the _____ bells all morning.
2. She really knew how _____ with problems.
3. Her _____ teacher was pleased with her audition.
4. _____ well at all times was her goal.
5. Our friends were _____ in Europe last month.
6. _____ diligently should produce a good grade.
7. Ben's father is a _____ man, always courteous and thoughtful.

PRACTICE D. Underline the verbals and the verbal phrases.
1. A raging storm is threatening the entire county.
2. Many frantic people have been calling the authorities to ask what to do.
3. Asking for help is a sensible act.
4. The authorities thought one caller's manner was enchanting, but her story was depressing.
5. To listen quietly required amazing patience from the officer who answered the phone.
6. Providing information has been an outstanding activity of the bureau.
7. Now the fading storm is leaving our area, and people will be able to return to their normal pursuits.

UNIT 14
Punctuation—Part I

REVIEW   The **comma** is the most frequently used—and abused—mark of punctuation.

Use the comma before a coordinating conjunction that separates two equal clauses.

> This job pays well, but the stress is unbearable.

Short clauses separated by *and* may omit the comma.

> She is alert and she is bright.

Always use the comma before the conjunction *but*.

> She is young, but she is experienced.

Use the comma after introductory words, phrases, and clauses.

> Nevertheless, the work must be done.
> Running to catch the bus, Leonard slipped on the ice.
> Until the bell has rung, you may relax.

Use the comma to separate items (words, phrases, and clauses) in a series.

> The office was decorated in purple, silver, and black.

> He works hard at home, on the job, and even during his vacation.

> The new employee complained that the hours were long, the pay was low, the work was boring, and the foreman was unfair.

Use commas around intervening words or before modifiers at the end of the sentence (such as appositives, nouns, or noun phrases of explanation).

His dinner, hot and appetizing, was set before him.

This report, quite different from the one you saw last week, is very detailed.

Walt Whitman was, indeed, a genius.

The river flowed before us, peaceful and quiet.

Eddie, my youngest brother, has become a champion, an Olympic gold-medalist.

Use the comma to set off nonrestrictive clauses (clauses that are not essential to the meaning of the sentence).

The Bristol County Renaissance Faire, which has been offered for many summers, will open on Sunday.

Marina Johnston, whom you met last summer, will arrive for the conference next week and will serve as moderator.

PRACTICE A. Punctuate the following sentences.
1. As you said the opening time is at noon.
2. Eight couples heading for the lake this morning went in three cars.
3. Not only do we plan to swim but we will also play tennis.
4. Apparently the shortcut is not a well-known route.
5. Be sure to bring a tablecloth napkins silverware and china.
6. Professor Lessing who wrote the book you read last week will give the main address at graduation.
7. Swimming like a fish Lonnie started on the last lap of his long swim.

REVIEW   The **semicolon**, a strong mark of punctuation, creates a solid pause in a sentence. Correct use of the semicolon adds a polished tone to writing.

Use the semicolon between two independent clauses that have a close relationship but are not connected by a comma and a coordinating conjunction.

> One restaurant on the west side of town employs a French chef; another cafe nearby utilizes the services of an Asian cook.

The semicolon is often used with the conjunctive adverb.

> They chose fifteen good men to be on the new steering committee; however, they were faulted for not including a few women.

The semicolon is used in a sentence that has other internal marks of punctuation.

> Holding out his arms, Gary waited happily for her; and we could sense his excitement.

PRACTICE B. As appropriate, punctuate the following sentences with semicolons. Add commas if necessary.

1. Their first trip took them to the Far East the second will take them to South America.
2. The Waltons have traveled all over the world consequently they cope well with all situations that develop while away from home.
3. Waiting beside the car, Erin and Caitlin watched the plane spin out of control they continued to watch it crash.
4. Her alarm did not ring therefore Tasha was late for class.
5. The first half of the game was disappointing the second half was even more so.

6. They ordered shrimp soup steak and salad they did not have any dessert.
7. Todd thinks he can make faster time on those back roads but I doubt it however he is the driver and can choose whatever route he likes.

PRACTICE C. Punctuate the following sentences.

1. As always her written work is concise clear and critical
2. We have invited Leeann her brother is the new editor to the dinner on Saturday evening for your father
3. Mario has ordered a new mower for the lake house but he will not receive it for three months
4. Since the weather has changed we will cancel our evening at the outdoor theater
5. Many busy people neglect their health consequently they pay the high price of ulcers strokes or heart attacks
6. Running daily Dave has maintained his good physical condition exercised the dog at the same time and made friends in the neighborhood he has also influenced others to join him
7. Mayor Stockwell stubborn and unconvinced would not change the budget regardless of the Board's criticism

REVIEW Use the **colon** to present information. It precedes:
Lists
Tabulations
Material to be emphasized
Examples or clarification
Restatements
Formal quotations
Details to expand a general statement

You will be meeting three people: Jean Smith, Ray Jones, and Cile Conner.

The situation can be described in one word: tense.

Gibran said: "There are no distances in remembering."

REVIEW   **Quotation marks** are used to enclose chapter headings, slang or coined words, and titles of articles, short stories, and short poems.

Always place the period and the comma inside the quotation marks.

The quotation mark and the exclamation point should be outside the quotation marks unless those marks of punctuation are part of the quotation.

Did Mother say "Dinner is ready"?
Mother asked, "Is dinner ready?"
That film was a "bummer"!
Sean said, "That record is a great one!"

PRACTICE D. As appropriate, punctuate the following sentences with colons or quotation marks.

1. Uncle Harris has four choices for his vacation Texas, New York, Washington, or the backyard!
2. For this cake, you will need these ingredients flour, sugar, eggs, milk, and vanilla.
3. Our new textbook has a chapter called Dream Interpretation.
4. Walter had one outstanding trait honesty.
5. My best friend always says, This, too, shall pass.
6. For a short period of time, her friends called everything that was good tough.
7. One of the short stories has the title Reaction; the other, The Red Rose.

PRACTICE E. Punctuate the following sentences as necessary.
1. Norman is a versatile person artist writer and singer
2. Be sure to include the following items on your sheet paper pens a ruler and highlighters.
3. I heard Faith ask Joan Could you come for lunch today?
4. When you find your book be sure to put your name and address on the title page.
5. Louisa has been studying hard every day therefore she should do well on the test.
6. On the other hand the politician may be completely honest but I doubt it.
7. The author quiet and shy has a quality the publisher admired determination

UNIT 15
Punctuation—Part II

REVIEW   This unit continues your review of marks of punctuation.

Use the **comma** to separate a series of three or more items.

> They brought us oranges, grapefruit, and persimmons from Florida.
> For the camping trip, we will need many supplies, including food, clothing, dishes, cooking pots, a first-aid kit, a tent, and sleeping bags.

Formal writing uses the comma in a series of only three items, but informal writing may omit the comma before *and*.

Use commas between coordinate adjectives. These adjectives have an equal relationship to the noun they modify.

> Brenda was a typical cheerleader—popular, extroverted, friendly, outgoing.
> Louann had a sunny, bright, sparkling personality.

Caution!   Do not use commas between non-coordinate adjectives, those that are unequal modifiers of the noun.

> Mr. White was an unhappy thin old man.
> Suddenly we could see the large white brick house.

Note: To help distinguish between coordinate and non-coordinate adjectives, substitute *and* in place of the comma. If it seems a reasonable statement, then the adjectives may be considered coordinate.

Do not separate adjectives of color, size, shape, and age by commas.

REVIEW Use the **hyphen** with compound adjectives, certain prefixes, and two-word numbers.

> bare-bones budget pro-Emerson
> low-flying plane ex-wife
> one-way ticket twenty-four days
> fifty-four-page report

Use the hyphen to join words for a special purpose and for coined words.

> devil-may-care look
> clickety-clackety-clockety sound

Note: An *ly* adverb used with an adjective is usually written without the hyphen.

> the completely exhausted woman
> the newly married Jon Baker

PRACTICE A. Punctuate the following sentences.

1. Senator Wilson was a bombastic old fellow with a one track mind.
2. Marilee was given a two hour deadline for the fourth edition.
3. Mrs. Brown, who lives next door, is an ex wrestler.
4. Janine's special friend was a green eyed blonde.
5. Her wink had a you're in this with me meaning.
6. The motor of the twin's car emits a strange chucky chucky choky sound.
7. Each morning Mitch makes a sixty second dash for the train.

Two hyphens make a dash:—. Use it infrequently. A formal use of the dash sets off a parenthetical insertion that requires an abrupt change of thought by the reader.

Today we will dissect a mud puppy—Jack, are you listening?—and then a frog.
The air controllers' strike began some days ago—it ruined our vacation plans, of course—and is an illegal action by those federal employees.

The dash may also precede a word or words that require emphasis.

One word could describe that man—terrific!
She wanted only one thing—complete devotion.

REVIEW One special use of the **parentheses** is to set off extra material that is not part of the main thought but closely related to it.

Our house in Muncie (perhaps you recall seeing it) has finally been sold.
The new store (one in a chain owned by a national organization) will open next month.

REVIEW Use **underlining** in handwritten or typed copy to replace italics. The following items should be underlined:

Titles of books, plays, films, operas, paintings, symphonic compositions, long poems and other complete works, periodicals, and newspapers

Names of ships, trains, aircraft
Names of legal cases
Scientific names
Foreign words
Words to be emphasized (do so infrequently)
Letters, numbers, and words used in a reference:

Example: The poster had an <u>A</u> and a <u>7</u> at the top.

PRACTICE B. Punctuate the following sentences.

1. You have one extra special asset courtesy.
2. Bib Bart's son is a student although he is now in Oklahoma City at SMU.
3. Susie has corresponded with fourteen friends not all at the same time of course in eight different countries.
4. A sensible hiker should wear stout walking shoes and comfortable loose fitting clothes in short forget the city sophistication.
5. Abou Ben Adam is the name of a short poem that my sister learned in the fourth grade.
6. Summerfest a special time of food and music in Chicago did not interest my friends museums for them!
7. The quiet gentle child was admired by her friends.

PRACTICE C. Punctuate the following sentences.

1. We're leaving no, no we'll be back at dawn tomorrow.
2. The Victorian period 1837–1901 was an unusual time of social economic and literary activity.
3. The dog had a come and get it attitude.
4. Mussolini was pro Nazi in his beliefs.
5. The Titanic, a ship that sank years ago, has been found in the waters off Newfoundland.
6. The law clerk has filed twenty one complaints.
7. Julia has an outstanding quality that we admire honesty.

UNIT 16
Phrases and Clauses

REVIEW   **Phrases** and **clauses** are units of words used in constructing sentences.

A phrase is a group of words that are related.

Noun phrases	the narrow brown pen a thin crescent moon
Prepositional phrases	under the bush around the bend up the shiny golden pole
Verbal phrases	choosing to meet the challenge to hear the bell
Verb phrases	is singing softly runs smoothly and silently

A clause is also a group of words that are related, but the clause is different because it contains a subject (S) and a verb (V).

(S)   (V)   (V)
Summer will soon be here.

(S) (V)   (V)
We are planting our garden tomorrow.

PRACTICE A. Mark **Ph** or **Cl** at the right to identify the following groups of words as **Ph**rases or **Cl**auses.
1. Bettina finished her paper last night   _____
2. Tossing his hat into the air   _____
3. Cutting and scraping and putting all the vegetables into a large black pot   _____
4. "Hurt not others with that which pains yourself"   _____
5. To undermine the moral fabric of this country   _____

6. Rushing along the river with a
   small canoe _____

7. Mr. Bell, your invention is a mixed
   blessing _____

PRACTICE B. Mark **Ph** or **Cl** at the right to identify the following
groups of words as **Ph**rases or **Cl**auses.

1. Below the steps of the front porch _____
2. Each child had to bring a rug to nap on _____
3. After an exciting shopping spree in
   London with Jean _____
4. Braided carefully by mountain women _____
5. Look at the bright colors in this one _____
6. Put it here _____
7. Controlling his energetic horse _____

REVIEW: Clauses are classified as **independent** or **dependent**.
An independent clause can stand alone; it is a complete
idea; it is a simple sentence.

> (S)   (V)
> Her dancing enchanted the audience.

> (S) (V) (V)
> A cold winter day can be dangerous.

A dependent clause, however, cannot stand alone as it
does not complete the idea of a sentence.

> (S) (V)
> Although he likes the format

> (S) (V)
> that he wants to finish

Dependent clauses are almost always introduced by
subordinating conjunctions or personal pronouns (*who,
whom*) or relative pronouns (*which, that*).

> since you spoke first
> whom you met
> that he said

Sometimes the introductory word is understood, just as the *you* is understood in the imperative mood of a verb:

Come here! (*You* is the understood subject.)

The book you want is
on the second shelf. (*that* you want)

That man you just
pushed is Reggie's uncle. (*whom* you just pushed)

Note: The introductory word may be omitted from the dependent clause if the omission does not confuse the reader.

PRACTICE C. Mark **I** or **D** at the right to identify **I**ndependent or **D**ependent clauses.
  1. When she was an elderly woman _____
  2. Since you love tennis _____
  3. Set up the pins again, please _____
  4. Underneath that black hat is a shock of red hair _____
  5. If the weather is right _____
  6. After you have written the paper _____
  7. Count me out _____

PRACTICE D. Mark **I** or **D** at the right to identify **I**ndependent or **D**ependent clauses.
  1. When you can _____
  2. Although you have chosen this course _____
  3. Yes, I will _____
  4. Could you move the sofa for me, please _____
  5. Which we could do quite easily _____
  6. Beyond the cars lay a van on its side _____
  7. Senator Browne has never accepted a bribe _____

UNIT 17
Kinds of Sentences

REVIEW   Four kinds of sentences add variety to writing and
speaking: **simple**, **compound**, **complex**, and
compound-complex. Each kind is determined by the
type and number of clauses included.

A **simple** sentence has one independent clause with a
subject and a verb. Either the subject or the verb or
both may be compound.

> The wind blew briskly all night.
> Betsy and Bruce stayed with us.
> Our dog whined, barked, and growled.
> Our children and our friends were laughing and
> shouting.

A **compound** sentence has two or more independent
clauses (IC) that are equal units in the sentence. The
clauses are connected by a comma and a coordinating
conjunction:

> Philip worked in the garden, but Beth stayed inside.

or by a semicolon:

> Philip worked in the garden; Beth stayed inside.
> Philip worked; Beth played; Brad prayed.

or by a conjunctive adverb and a semicolon:

> Jay wrecked the car; consequently, he was in serious
> trouble.

A **complex** sentence has one independent clause (IC)
and at least one dependent clause (DC). To be connected,
clauses should have a definite relationship to one another.

>   (DC)   (IC)
> When she put her foot on the brake, the car slowed
> quickly.

(IC)   (DC)   (DC)
He tried to tell her that she was right and that he was wrong.

A **compound-complex** sentence has two or more independent clauses and at least one dependent clause.

(IC)   (IC)
They wanted to go dancing, but they watched TV

(DC)
instead because they had no transportation.

(IC)   (IC)   (IC)
She liked Jack, she tolerated Jim, she loved Will;

(DC)   (IC)
however, when she chose her husband, she picked— Mark!

Note: When identifying an independent clause, omit the coordinating conjunction because the clauses are equal units.

Keats was a Romanticist poet, but Maya Angelou is a contemporary poet.

When identifying dependent clauses, retain the subordinating conjunction.

When Leah reads poetry, she "loses" reality.

Sometimes subordinating conjunctions are understood.

He likes the book Tomas wrote.   (understood *that*)
Marcelle wants the scarf you wove. (understood *which*)

For further clarification of coordinating and subordinating conjunctions, see Unit 8.

PRACTICE A. At the right, identify the sentences as <u>S</u>imple, <u>C</u>ompound, <u>C</u>omple<u>x</u> (**<u>CX</u>**), or <u>C</u>ompound-<u>C</u>omplex (**<u>CC</u>**).
1. She will meet us where the boulevard begins. _____
2. You may not believe it, but I am here to help you. _____
3. Yumi stayed at the camp for the rest of the work period. _____
4. Sarah and Harold bowled with Jackson last Saturday and skated with him on Sunday. _____
5. Although they lived near the park, they had never been there. _____
6. Beyond the snowcapped mountains lay a tiny village. _____
7. Not many poets can live on the income they receive from their writing; therefore, they often seek other forms of employment. _____

PRACTICE B. Identify the sentences as **<u>S</u>**, **<u>C</u>**, **<u>CX</u>**, **<u>CC</u>**.
1. The conference in New York brought together many people interested in peace. _____
2. Although fourteen languages could be heard, people seemed to understand each other, even without the interpreters. _____
3. Some groups brought their own language experts; others depended on the conference interpreters. _____
4. When they were not in session, they explored the city that offered diverse experiences. _____
5. Everyone visited the great lady in the harbor: the Statue of Liberty. _____
6. Some visitors found their way to the special museum, far from the heart of the city. _____

7. The educators in the group wanted to see all the great universities, and the artists were just as eager to lose themselves in the famous museums. _____

PRACTICE C. Identify the sentences as **S**, **C**, **CX**, **CC**.

1. When the weather is this cold, people should stay indoors. _____
2. Please bring the following items: buns, hamburgers, pickles, potato chips, and soda. _____
3. We will start for the camp at daybreak, but the others will leave at noon. _____
4. They will leave later because we will need to clean the cabins, and we will also have to shop for food. _____
5. Lisa has never met anyone as quiet or as thoughtful as Gina. _____
6. You may take this suitcase; however, leave that one for Harvey. _____
7. If the weather does not change, we will be confined to the house for a week. _____

Modifiers—Dangling and Misplaced

REVIEW   When **modifiers**, such as **participles**, **gerunds**, or **infinitives**, do not clearly refer to a specific word, they become dangling modifiers and confuse the meaning of the sentence.

Dangling Participles

> While driving, the car went out of control on a patch of ice.

Clarify *who* was driving.

> While I was driving, the car went out of control on a patch of ice.

> Visiting and relaxing, the holiday passed quickly.

Clarify that *you* were the active ones, *not* the holiday.

> As we visited and relaxed, the holiday passed quickly.

Dangling Gerunds

> In throwing a Frisbee well, practice and skill are useful.

Clarify that a *person* throws a Frisbee.

> In throwing a Frisbee well, a person needs practice and skill.

> After scolding the child, her anger subsided.

Clarify that *anger* did not scold the child.

> After she scolded the child, the mother's anger subsided.

Dangling Infinitives

> To do well in college, study and determination are helpful.

Clarify that a *person* is a college student.

> To do well in college, you must study and be determined.

> To own a coordinated wardrobe, careful shopping and planning are necessary.

Clarify the point that *people* plan wardrobes.

> To have a coordinated wardrobe, one must plan and shop carefully.

REVIEW   In **elliptical** clauses, a subject or predicate has been omitted. If a subject has been dropped, be sure that the subject of the independent clause and the meaning are clear.

> When only four, Andrew's *father* opened his own restaurant.

Clarify that it was not the *father* who was four.

> When Andrew was only four, his father opened his own restaurant.

> When only four, Andrew knew that his father had opened his own restaurant.

Caution!   Be alert to the ambiguities created by the use of adverbs such as *only, nearly, frequently,* and so on.

REVIEW If modifying words, phrases, and clauses are not placed as close as possible to the words they describe, they become **misplaced** modifiers and create awkward or absurd constructions.

> Regan *only* eats tomatoes from her garden.
> She eats nothing else?
> Regan eats *only* tomatoes from her garden.
> She eats nothing else from her garden?
> If true, the sentence is correct.

Misplaced Phrases

> They threw back the fish into the ocean, too small to keep.

Clarify the point that it is the *fish* that are too small, not the *ocean*.

> They threw back into the ocean the fish too small to keep.

> Spoiled and dangerous to eat, they tossed the meat into the green can.

Clarify the point that it is the *meat* that is spoiled and dangerous.

> They tossed the meat, spoiled and dangerous to eat, into the green can.

Misplaced Clauses

> Those books have been returned to the shelves that are first editions.

Clarify the point that the *books* are the first editions.

> Those books that are the first editions have been returned to the shelves.

Dad fed the dog on the back porch that seemed to be starving.

Clarify the point that it is the *dog* that seems to be starving.

Dad fed the dog that seemed to be starving.
or
On the back porch, Dad fed the dog that seemed to be starving.

PRACTICE A. Rewrite the following sentences for clarity.

1. Tossed into the salad, I saw six uncut onions.

   _____

2. Never serve pork to your family that has not been cooked well.

   _____

3. Sonny couldn't drive to his school with two sprained wrists.

   _____

4. The chair was given to us by our aunt with the velvet fringe.

   _____

5. I saw her car along the highway that was stalled.

   _____

6. We watched the active skaters sitting in the stands.

   _____

7. Laughing, talking, and hugging, our reunion was enjoyed.

   _____

PRACTICE B. Rewrite the following sentences for clarity.

1. Mrs. Stone only eats green beans from the Farmer's Market.

    _____

2. The saleswoman knocked loudly on our door with the long red hair.

    _____

3. To prepare good food, fresh ingredients and time are needed.

    _____

4. Thrown over the chair, Kristen found her jacket.

    _____

5. The client's mother died when she was six.

    _____

6. Grazing along the edge of the road, we saw three deer.

    _____

7. Rosa nearly bowled a perfect score.

    _____

UNIT 19

Sentence Errors

REVIEW   Three major errors in sentence construction are the sentence **fragment**, the **comma splice**, and the **run-on**.

A sentence fragment is a dependent clause or phrase used as a sentence. Sometimes a writer may include a "justifiable fragment" in written dialogue or in an explanation, for example, but more often, a fragment is simply an error, not a stylistic device.

> After they had shown us the film.
> Holding the prize.

A fragment can often be corrected by simply joining it to a sentence that precedes or follows it.

> After they had shown us the film, the crew was finished for the day.

> The young girl felt extremely happy holding the prize.

REVIEW   The comma splice and the run-on are sometimes called **comma faults**. Connecting independent clauses with a comma when a stronger mark of punctuation should be used creates a comma splice.

> Lewis served as foreman for the highway crew, his brother served as the paymaster for the construction company.

> Under the new rules, the student will design her own program, each program will then be approved by the Academic Dean.

To correct the comma splice, substitute a semicolon or divide the sentence into two separate sentences.

Lewis served as foreman for the highway crew; his brother served as the paymaster for the construction company.

Under the new rules, the student will design her own program. Each program will then be approved by the Academic Dean.

REVIEW   A **run-on** sentence has no punctuation between clauses where punctuation is required.

Laura and Ken came home with us but Andi and Glenn stayed in Baltimore.

Carol brought the books for the seminar she also brought three journal articles.

To correct a run-on, add a comma with the coordinating conjunction or add a semicolon, with or without a conjunctive adverb.

Laura and Ken come home with us, but Andi and Glenn stayed in Baltimore.

Carol brought the books for the seminar; she also brought three journal articles.

Note: Incorrect punctuation with the conjunctive adverb can create a comma splice and/or a run-on.

Comma Splice   Whatever plan of action you approve will be acceptable, however, our other friends will not be satisfied.

Run-On   Whatever plan of action you approve will be acceptable however, our other friends will not be satisfied.

To correct either of these sentences, use a semicolon and a comma.

> Whatever plan of action you approve will be acceptable; however, our other friends will not be satisfied.

PRACTICE A. Identify the following statements as a **S**entence **F**ragments (**SF**) or **C**omplete **S**entences (**CS**).

1. Louise certainly receives many telephone calls. _____
2. Having returned all the credit cards. _____
3. Your new car will be delivered today. _____
4. Bring the books today. _____
5. After he had written a note. _____
6. The writers have finished the play on time. _____
7. Running along the dry creek bed on the edge of the desert. _____

PRACTICE B. Identify the error in the following sentences as a **R**un-**O**n (**RO**) or a **C**omma **S**plice (**CS**).

1. Jonathan has arrived but Janna will not come until later. _____
2. You may serve the appetizers now, the entree can be served later. _____
3. The caterer is expensive, however, the food is superb. _____
4. After dinner is over we will hear an exciting program. _____
5. Two mimes will entertain us first and then a group from the college will play for us to dance. _____
6. Join us as soon as you can however, we hope you can get here by ten. _____
7. Today's activity is only part of the celebration and tomorrow will bring another full day of fun. _____

PRACTICE C. Identify the error in each sentence as a **R**un-**O**n (**RO**), **C**omma **S**plice (**CS**), or **S**entence **F**ragment (**SF**).

1. Snow has been falling all day, consequently we have to shovel. _____
2. Snowing, really, since last night. _____
3. When we awakened early this morning. _____
4. The shrubs are flattened by the weight of the snow but the trees appear to be all right. _____
5. Because we were prepared for this storm by the weather news on all the TV channels. _____
6. Last year we had heavy snow but the year before we had a frightening blizzard. _____
7. We had plenty of food on hand however we needed milk, bread, and cat food. _____

UNIT 20

Clauses with Special Functions

REVIEW   This unit focuses on special clause identification.

Clauses can be used as nouns, adjectives, or adverbs.

A **noun clause** is in a noun position and functions as a noun.

> *What his purpose may be* is a mystery to us.
>   (Used as the subject.)

> I don't know *what his plan is*.
>   (Used as the direct object.)

> Give the award to *whoever was chosen by the class*.
>   (Used as the object of the preposition.)

An **adjective clause** acts as an adjective by modifying nouns and pronouns. For clarity, it follows the word it modifies. Because adjective clauses relate one idea to another, they are also called relative clauses.

> This is the dress *that I chose*.
> The person *whom you see* is Dad's business partner.
> Someone *who is tall* will be helpful to us.

When describing people, use *who* or *whom* (or *that,* in some instances).

When describing things, use *which* or *that*.

> The director *who is new* will help you with your work.
> Mr. Berkson is the man *whom I introduced* at the meeting.
> There is the car *that I bought*.

An **adverbial clause** acts as an adverb by modifying verbs, adjectives, or other adverbs.

When the storm started, she was frantic.

She worried *because her son was late.*

For once he felt brave, *which was an enviable emotion.*

Many people were sad *because their favorite leader had died.*

When the emergency call came, they naturally left for the hospital, and quickly, too.

She acted bravely, *although the pain was intense.*

REVIEW

A clause that is necessary to the meaning of the sentence is called a **restrictive clause**.

His car is the one *that has been repainted.*
The house *that was blown down yesterday* belongs to my uncle.

Caution!

Do not use commas with restrictive clauses.

A clause that is not necessary to the meaning of a sentence is nonrestrictive and is set off by commas.

Our vacation, which was a welcome diversion, lasted a month.

Our friends, who are very dear to us, arrive today to attend the awards ceremony with our family.

Examinations will be given, whether you're ready or not.

Note:

Noun clauses are restrictive. Adjective (relative) and adverbial clauses can be either restrictive or nonrestrictive.

PRACTICE A. Underline noun, adjective (relative), or adverbial clauses in the following sentences and identify at the right.

1. What you have heard is true. _____

2. The judges heard only what they wanted to hear. _____

3. Her arm throbbed because she had burned her wrist. _____

4. These flowers are the ones that John sent. _____

5. Match the china to whichever tablecloth you prefer. _____

6. The coat that Julie bought will be perfect to wear to the reception. _____

7. When I left the house, I saw my friend walking down the street. _____

PRACTICE B. Underline noun, adjective (relative), or adverbial clauses in the following sentences and identify at the right.

1. While Dad slept, my brother mowed the lawn. _____

2. The poem that you wrote should please your editor very much. _____

3. Mr. Brown sent what you ordered. _____

4. The plan that you intend to introduce will not be acceptable to the Board of Trustees. _____

5. What has just happened should not affect your decision. _____

6. No, it is definitely not the book that Dan ordered. _____

7. You will find the keys where you left them yesterday. _____

PRACTICE C. Underline the restrictive and nonrestrictive clauses. Identify them at the right and punctuate the sentences correctly.

1. According to some experts, children who have temper tantrums should be ignored. _____
2. Our friends will call whether you think so or not. _____
3. The bread which was baked in a conventional oven is made with four kinds of flour. _____
4. This brief which Molly prepared is written extremely well. _____
5. That you have chosen this course of action suggests a stubborn attitude. _____
6. Mrs. Jackdaw whom you met last week will chair the United Fund Committee. _____
7. Barnaby has a new car that Amy covets! _____

PRACTICE D. Underline the restrictive and nonrestrictive clauses. Identify them at the right and punctuate the sentences correctly.

1. Dogs who bite strangers may be bad-tempered or have had special training! _____
2. Her flowers which won first prize at the Garden Club Show were a wonderful mixture of roses, mums, dahlias, phlox, marigolds, begonias, and petunias. _____
3. Toby wanted to know why you left the meeting last Sunday. _____
4. Whom you wish to believe is your choice. _____
5. When you're tense a light TV program can relax you. _____
6. He is curious about why you were there. _____
7. Mother who studied music in Billings has been teaching in a nursing program. _____

UNIT 21

Coordination and Subordination

REVIEW **Coordination**, the joining of words and ideas of equal value, reinforces emphasis and logical relationships.

> *The new books have been shelved in the library,* and *now the students can use them.*

> *Mr. Strom has donated four desks for the use of student editors,* and *Mr. Jones has sent a check to be used as the students wish.*

> *Her cousin likes apple pie,* but *her uncle prefers apple fritters.*

Phrased this way, the two ideas in each sentence have equal importance.

Note: Review compound sentences in Unit 17 and punctuation in Units 14 and 15.

Caution! Used excessively, coordination contributes to a choppy, childish, and ineffective style of writing. Used appropriately, coordination strengthens clear writing.

REVIEW **Subordination** is also used to show a logical and clear relationship between ideas, especially when time, place, or cause and effect are involved. The *idea* in the independent clause is emphasized more than the one in the dependent clause or indicates an important sequence.

> *When the rain came,* the party on the beach ended.

> *Although he sent his application in April,* he did not receive the good news of acceptance until the middle of July.

> Six boys will stay here for the three-day vacation *because their homes are 3,000 miles away.*

He has promised to meet you on the corner *where you catch your bus.*

Subordinating conjunctions, such as *after, although, before, because, since, while,* and *if,* head the list of dependent clauses. (For further review, refer to Unit 8.)

Note: Review the use of commas after introductory phrases in Unit 14.

Caution! Used excessively, subordination weakens writing style. Used well, subordination becomes a significant element in the effective presentation of ideas.

PRACTICE A. Underline independent (coordinate) or dependent (subordinate) clauses and identify them over the first word of each clause. At the right, mark whether coordination or subordination has been used.

1. Their ideas were good, but they will not be used. _____
2. Since you visited our fair city, we have seen many changes. _____
3. The books were sold to the students before classes began. _____
4. Her garden, which was truly beautiful, won the first prize. _____
5. If the weather is favorable, we will go to the outdoor concert. _____
6. The Village Manager has submitted her budget for the next year, and the Board has approved it. _____
7. The man whom you need for that committee is Blaine Thomas. _____

PRACTICE B. Write seven sentences that use the principles of coordination and subordination.

1. _____
2. _____
3. _____
4. _____
5. _____
6. _____
7. _____

PRACTICE C. Underline independent (coordinate) or dependent (subordinate) clauses and identify them over the first word of each clause. At the right, mark whether coordination or subordination has been used.

1. Since the humidity is high, let's stay indoors where it's cool. _____

2. You may choose this color for your bedspread and draperies; or, if you like, select another that pleases you more. _____

3. After the concert ended, we walked to the restaurant. _____

4. Your art supplies have not been shipped because a strike at the factory has delayed production. _____

5. As you know, the election that year caused repercussions that are still evident today. _____

6. She has spent hours on her project, yet it will not be ready on time. _____

7. Ray will drive Dad's car, and you can take Keesha's truck, which handles easily, too. _____

Parallelism

REVIEW   **Parallelism** refers to the use of similar structures in a
sentence. When these structures are alike in length and
rhythm, the sentence is said to be balanced. Parallelism
can be developed, for example, by the use of repeated
words (such as nouns or prepositions) or phrases and
clauses, the same verb, or verbs that have the same
meaning.

> **Parallel Nouns**   Both effort and perseverance will
> bring rewards.
>
> **Parallel**   Jackie is creative but unpredictable.
> **Adjectives**
>
> **Parallel**   Mark wanted to swim, to ski, and to
> **Infinitives**   run in the Olympics.
>
> **Exact Balance**   It is true that you may fool all of the
> **and**   people some of the time; you can
> **Parallelism**   even fool some of the people all of
> the time; but you can't fool all of
> the people all of the time.
>
> *—Abraham Lincoln*

Note: A degree of parallelism adds interest, clarity, and variety
to writing by emphasizing ideas or by showing how
ideas are alike or different.

Caution!   Be sure the relationship of the ideas warrants parallelism. Consider the text.

Since parallelism is a form of coordination, parallel sentence elements must be equal.

Be especially careful when using the correlative conjunctions, both . . . and, either . . . or, neither . . . nor, and so on. (Refer to Unit 8.)

> **Incorrect**   Lucinda not only invited all her family but also all his family.

The verb and noun phrases that follow the conjunctions are not parallel.

> **Correct**   Lucinda not only invited all her family but also invited all his family.

> **Incorrect**   We communicated with our families either by letters or sending postcards.

Either is followed by a prepositional phrase, but *or* is followed by a verbal phrase.

> **Correct**   We communicated with our families either by letters or by postcards.

Now two prepositional phrases follow the conjunctions, and the sentence is parallel.

Note: Attention to the technique of parallelism helps the writer to eliminate careless shifts from one construction to a dissimilar one and to avoid unbalanced constructions. (Refer to Unit 3 and Unit 12.)

PRACTICE A. Correct any errors in parallelism by underlining the error and then rewriting the sentence to make it parallel.

1. My hobbies are knitting, reading, and to take long hikes.

   _____

   _____

2. Bobbie was singing and washed dishes at the same time.

   _____

   _____

3. They wanted to head for the beach and for a swim.

   _____

   _____

4. We want mature people and who are experienced.

   _____

   _____

5. Their dogs are friendly, disciplined, and have good "manners."

   _____

   _____

6. We have always found him courteous as the man, learned as the lawyer, and is creative as a thinker.

   _____

   _____

7. The people hope for a mayor who is honest, who is reliable, and is a Republican.

   _____

   _____

PRACTICE B. Correct any errors in parallelism by underlining the error and then rewriting the sentence to make it parallel.

1. Consequently, the car was smashed, looted, and then fire burned it beyond repair.

    _____

    _____

2. Our patients are trying to walk, developing new muscles, and to become self-reliant.

    _____

    _____

3. Leo will neither drink tea nor coffee.

    _____

    _____

4. Amanda enjoyed visiting all the cities, touring the cathedrals and museums, and to shop in all the elegant stores.

    _____

    _____

5. The president was loved by the Democrats, hated by the Republicans, but the voters simply tolerated him.

    _____

    _____

6. Writing stories was easy for O. Henry, but to write stories would be difficult for me.

    _____

    _____

7. Mother warned us about the danger at the quarry and that we could get into serious trouble if we swam alone.

    _____

    _____

PRACTICE C. Rewrite the following sentences to eliminate awkward shifts in tense or voice.

1. When the doorbell rang, I went to the door, but no one is there

   _____

   _____

2. After the guests seated themselves at the table, a bowl of soup was served to them.

   _____

   _____

3. If Jeff is rude to him, his father scolded him.

   _____

   _____

4. After the new film had been criticized so extensively, we decided not to see it.

   _____

   _____

5. The student left the room quickly, but he was stopped by the teacher.

   _____

   _____

6. We have listed the objectives of our program, but the students have still been unsure about the methods to use.

   _____

   _____

7. After we served dinner, we have gone out to the terrace for coffee.

   _____

   _____

Post-Test

1. Underline all nouns.
   a. When summer comes, students scatter in all directions; some attend classes; they vacation; they have fun; they take jobs; they indulge in dreams.
   b. Their families enjoy having more time together and opportunities to share new experiences in travel.

2. Underline the subject nouns.
   a. Beneath the Great Barrier Reef lie amazing coral formations and foliage.
   b. Moving slowly over the water, a large excursion boat carries any passengers to enjoy the beauty of the reef.
   c. Interestingly, the coastline is also fascinating.
   d. The chefs in the gallery and the stewards cook and serve a delicious luncheon on each trip.
   e. Only a few passengers suffer from seasickness because the waters of the reef are calm.

3. Underline all pronouns.
   a. She told each student that no one could be late with his or her papers, which made an impression on those individuals.
   b. They told me nothing would keep them from meeting their deadlines.

4. Underline all verbs.
   a. Our friends were flying to England today, then taking the "Chunnel" to France, and staying in Paris for a long weekend before they left for Zurich.
   b. They have not traveled on the Continent before, so they have been truly happy about this opportunity.
   c. They intend to visit Switzerland and Austria; after seeing those countries, they will explore the Riviera.

5. Underline all adjectives.

a. Bob's company, quite large, has been setting an impressive level of international sales for even the strongest competitors.
b. The lengthy push for foreign marketers has been difficult, but wise decisions and careful marketing have been rewarding for his salesmen.

6. Underline all adverbs.
   a. The two teams are fairly matched; the coach is very sure of it.
   b. They will leave early because the first game usually has been scheduled at ten o'clock.
   c. One of the teams has quite a strong chance of success because it is truly experienced.
   d. One player has always been a daringly bold kicker, which will help the team.
   e. It is not hard to imagine a fiercely contested match.
   f. We are really hoping to have good news later.

7. Underline all prepositions or prepositional phrases.
   a. What do you want Jem for? He's in the library studying for that math test at noon today.
   b. Under any circumstances, exams are a test of Jem's patience and ability to review his notes in a sensible way.
   c. When Jem sits down for a test in the classroom, he puts his lucky charm on the desk.
   d. He organizes his pens and pencils between his candy and his soda.
   e. Underneath his calm exterior, Jem is tense but ready!

8. Underline all conjunctions.
   a. Both the coach and the players have agreed to work together and bury all their differences.
   b. When they arrive in Boston, they will choose the referee because it is their responsibility now.
   c. The other team will also approve their choice; therefore, everyone should be satisfied, and harmony can reign.

d. Since all teams will be in Boston for a week, plenty of time will be available for sightseeing and recreation.

e. Neither the pressure nor the competition of the tournament has been overlooked, but we know they will try their best to win.

9. Underline all interjections.
   a. Look this way, Brent!
   b. Wait! The photographer is not ready.
   c. You may have—yes!—two pictures.
   d. Have you seem them now? They're perfect!

10. Underline all phrases.
    a. Swinging her feet over the edge of the pool, Bonita felt as if she were a real part of the Hollywood scene.
    b. To tell the truth, she was misguided by her poor judgment.
    c. Bonita's judgment had not been helped by advice given from inexperienced friends who wanted to control her decisions.
    d. She liked acting in films.
    e. Performing on stage had been her passion for years while growing up in a small town.

11. Identify the following as **Ph**rase or **Cl**ause.
    a. swinging back and forth on the tire was a young chimp _____
    b. in the middle of the monkey island _____
    c. children like to see the penguins _____
    d. although the elephants performed nobly _____
    e. two tigers, roaring at all of us _____
    f. close to its mother was tucked a baby rhino _____

12. Identify the following clauses as **I**ndependent or **D**ependent.
    a. under the book on the table lay the missing letter _____
    b. when he was asked by either the police, the attorney, or his family, or his friends _____
    c. could he have misinterpreted the message _____
    d. as he checked the situation, face grave, manner intense, and attitude confrontational _____

13. Identify verbs in the following sentences as **Tr**ansitive,
    Intransitive, or **L**inking.
    a. After all the excitement at the theater last night,
        the family could not sleep.   _____
    b. The British actor, composed and haughty, had
        been their favorite for years.   _____
    c. They had seen his picture on the colorful posters
        in the lobby.   _____
    d. However, to actually meet him was a thrill!   _____
    e. They were still humming with pleasure about the
        introduction.   _____
    f. The family will never forget this special experience.   _____

14. Correct any shifts in tense or voice of the verb.
    a. When Aiko saw the teacher handing out the tests, he knows
        his moment of reckoning has come.

        _____

        _____

    b. His test was put in his hand, but he was not ready to look at
        the grade.

        _____

        _____

15. Underline the verbals in each sentence and identify as **G**erund,
    Participle, or **Inf**initive.
    a. On his birthday, the delighted child wanted to
        stay up all night!   _____

    b. Opening his presents was the most fun he had
        had in a long time.   _____

    c. To please him, his mother allowed him two more
        hours past his usual chosen bedtime.   _____

    d. Building castles with his new blocks kept him busy.   _____

    e. He would not allow anyone to help him.   _____

    f. The pleased child was finally carried off to bed.   _____

16. Underline the subject with one line and the verb with two lines.
    a. Beyond the street lights loomed threatening shadows.
    b. Inside the house, gusts of wind made the family nervous.

    Underline the direct objects.
    a. He has accepted her as his peer in all activities.
    b. Unquestionably, the two have tried every possible solution for the problem.

    Underline the indirect object.
    a. Could you tell me the time, please?
    b. Finally, they have offered us new clocks for all the rooms.

    Underline and identify the **P**redicate **N**oun (**PN**) or the **P**redicate **A**djective (**PA**).

    a. That western town is a veritable ghost town, deserted by all but an inquisitive lizard or two and clumps of tumbleweeds.

    b. Its atmosphere is truly somewhat frightening to a visitor.

17. Correct any misplaced or dangling modifiers in the following sentences.
    a. Walking along the beach, the moon was a silver crescent that sparkled.

    _____

    _____

    b. We joined the others sitting on the sand in the blazing fire.

    _____

    _____

    c. To build a special beach fire, skill and lots of firewood are very helpful.

    _____

    _____

    d. While singing, the fire made it comfortable in the cool wind that blew in off the water.

    _____

    _____

   e. Hanging low in the night sky, we were dazzled by the brilliant stars that looked immense.

_____

_____

18. Identify the following sentences as **S**imple, **C**ompound, **C**omple**x** (**CX**), or **C**ompound-**C**omplex (**CC**).
   a. Glacier National Park offers many sightseeing "treasures."   _____
   b. For example, one can see a real glacier that lies just across a small body of water in front of a lodge.   _____
   c. Some visitors have seen twelve elk marching across the road, which is quite surprising.   _____
   d. High in the mountains can be seen a number of wild animals; rock formations are equally interesting.   _____
   e. Many young people who attend various colleges and universities work in park lodges; they celebrate Christmas in July.   _____
   f. Yes, they have Christmas in July with decorated trees, carols, presents—and merriment.   _____

19. Identify the following sentences as **A**ctive or **P**assive.
   a. Have you ever gone to Door County, Wisconsin, for a vacation?   _____
   b. Many special attractions have been created there.   _____
   c. One feature that pleases hungry people is a fish boil.   _____
   d. The fish boil is prepared in front of a huge audience.   _____
   e. Some people eat the fish fast so they can get to the delicious cherry pie on their trays.   _____
   f. If you have the opportunity, go to Door County and don't miss the ice cream cones at Wilson's in Ephraim.   _____

20. Correct any non-parallel sentence elements.
    a. We need an actor who is experienced, talented, **and who is** cooperative.

    _____

    _____

    b. The actor's role may involve his singing, **dancing, and to** train the chorus.

    _____

    _____

21. Correct any faulty coordination or subordination.
    a. The children went outside for recess **when the whistle** sounded.

    _____

    _____

    b. Some of the youngsters played ball, **and some raced around,** and some played on the swings.

    _____

    _____

22. Identify all sentence errors as **F**ragment, **R**un-**O**n (**RO**), or **C**omma-**S**plice (**CS**).
    a. One brother, working on bridges in Brazil.   _____
    b. Luke also has a sister, she serves as a **nurse at a** veterans hospital.   _____
    c. We know Chan visited her last May but **he didn't** stay very long.   _____
    d. Hoping against hope for a return visit.   _____
    e. Chan bought a ticket for Luke, **however he has** not used it.   _____
    f. Did you know that Luke and Chan are **twins and** they have lived here for only three years?   _____

23. Punctuate the following sentences.
    a. Please let us help you with your program we are eager to help
    b. We can offer the services of Jenna Julie and Jackson but we'll need an answer soon
    c. Its easy for us to rearrange Mikes schedule if you would like us to do so
    d. If you can give us a deadline by Friday it will help us
    e. We have experience with this type of effort therefore you would benefit from our participation
    f. We will e-mail our suggestions to you tomorrow and you can respond the same way

24. a. Define a topic sentence.

    _____

    _____

    b. Define a thesis statement.

    _____

    _____

Answer Key: Pre-Test

Exercise 1
    a. student, class, field trip
    b. Carmen Lopez, teacher, charge
    c. bus
    d. seat, belts, person

Exercise 2
    a. students
    b. phone or cell phone
    c. horses
    d. barricade
    e. barricade

Exercise 3
    a. you, your
    b. it, anyone
    c. My, us, they
    d. We, our
    e. I, myself, them

Exercise 4
    a. flew, went
    b. had, searched
    c. have had
    d. waded, swam
    e. shrieked, washed
    f. will show

Exercise 5
    a. brilliant, beautiful
    b. Violet, pink, gray
    c. bright, dark
    d. eastern, soft, white
    e. lovely, welcome

Exercise 6
a. very
b. not, easily, too
c. outstandingly
d. slowly, carefully
e. soon, truly
f. cautiously, not, dangerously

Exercise 7
a. In the park, of children, from . . . lot
b. under . . . trees, with craft kits
c. on . . . courts, between . . . buildings
d. by . . . boys, in . . . shorts
e. Beside . . . beds, underneath . . . statue, on . . . grass

Exercise 8
a. or
b. but
c. both—and, and
d. However, and
e. since, either, or
f. therefore, and

Exercise 9
a. Oh no
b. Watch . . . Jordan!
c. please!
d. look . . . play!

Exercise 10
a. at . . . School, to . . . D.C., in May
b. Helping . . . details
c. Checking . . . hotel, on arrival, in the city, at six o'clock
d. to begin their tour, of the city
e. of . . . Wall
f. To visit Congress, for . . . students, from Wilson

Exercise 11
   a. Ph
   b. Cl
   c. Ph
   d. Ph
   e. Cl
   f. Ph

Exercise 12
   a. D
   b. I
   c. D
   d. I

Exercise 13
   a. L
   b. Intr
   c. Intr
   d. L
   e. Tr
   f. Tr

Exercise 14
   a. will take
   b. he will appreciate . . .

Exercise 15
   a. exciting—P
   b. running . . . another—G
   c. to do first—Inf
   d. riding the airplanes—G
   e. to have . . . possible—Inf
   f. tantalizing—P

Exercise 16

a. S—rabbits, chipmunk
    V—lived
b. S—trio
    V—played

a. assistance
b. thief

a. for his grandmother
b. her

a. PA—comfortable, confident
b. PN—Congressman

Exercise 17

a. Crawling . . . dunes, Lucy . . .
b. When Lucy was . . .
c. you need discipline and effort
d. buckles hanging . . . waist
e. When you are in . . .

Exercise 18

a. CX
b. S
c. CX
d. C
e. S
f. CC

Exercise 19

a. P
b. P
c. A
d. A
e. P
f. A

Exercise 20
    a. how to organize
    b. hiking

Exercise 21
    a. play at the end of the week.
    b. When they . . ., the other . . .

Exercise 22
    a. F
    b. RO
    c. F
    d. CS
    e. CS/RO
    f. F

Exercise 23
    a. alike,
    b. Grace, Edna,
    c. cats, dogs, birds; however,
    d. hobby: sports
    e. Kim, "Painting . . . do."
    f. you listen—quiet, please—to . . . announcement.

Exercise 24
    a. A topic sentence introduces the idea of a paragraph.
    b. A thesis statement presents the major idea of a paper (essay, etc.).

Answer Key: Practices

Unit 1, page 9
A.
1. justice, truth, keystones, concept, law, United States
2. Betsy, Bert, length, trip, Belgium, fall
3. ideas, archaeologists, exodus, tribes, plains
4. men, women, game, tennis
5. Jenna's (used as adjective), song, thing, beauty, joy
6. recipes, cookbook, rice, sauce, casseroles, quality
7. matinee, event, children, adults

B. Suggestions
1. Mother, books
2. Marie, cookies
3. essays, poems
4. teacher, Jack, Cile, Ray

C.
1. Bob, garden, hours, tomatoes, squash, beans
2. corner, caravan, campers, sizes, kinds
3. company (used as adjective), lot (or parking lot as a unit), people, hours
4. plans, picnic, people, show, Saturday
5. campers, group, children, students, women, businessmen, cowboys
6. Rod, parade, people, work, vacationers
7. day, relaxation, fun, highlights, crowd

Unit 2, page 11
A.
1. excursion boat
2. car
3. ring
4. players
5. Lesley, Raymond
6. newspaper
7. envelope

B. Suggestions
1. Jack, Jill
2. woman
3. children
4. Pat, Bill, Gina

C.

1. dogs, cats
2. cat
3. puppy
4. heart

5. animals
6. Mutt, Jeff
7. cat

Unit 3, page 13
A.

1. howled, whistled
2. can do, have tried
3. hoped
4. is

5. seems, are
6. is, are
7. were humming, singing

B. Suggestions
1. shouted
2. eat, drink
3. hikes, skates, bowls
4. saw, hit

C.

1. enjoyed
2. jumped, played, built
3. were, felt
4. stretched out (verbal idiom), yawned

5. had
6. can imagine
7. rested

D.

1. tense (asked) asks
2. voice (were eaten) she has eaten
3. voice (has been enjoyed) he has also enjoyed
4. tense (write) wrote

E.
1. tense (is) was
2. voice (was predicted) they predicted
3. voice (had been left) some parents left
4. tense (listen) listened

Unit 4, page 19

A.

1. they, we, some
2. our, all
3. that, she, her
4. us, we, it, who
5. this, one, you, your, first, second
6. anyone, that, someone, it
7. those, him, they

B. Suggestions
1. himself, four, their
2. You, our
3. five, he, them
4. two, one, those

C.

1. anyone, her
2. first, three, her, others
3. we, she, our
4. it, us, she, two, who, their
5. those, I, my, I, my
6. everyone, whose, who, which
7. your, mine, which, she

Unit 5, page 24

A.
1. large, great, many
2. Those, foolish, all, black, purple
3. that, violent, wide, old
4. colored, red, green, yellow, blue, young, acrobat's (adjectival)
5. her, charming, her, basic, her
6. sweet, soft, of Bach, our
7. beautiful, all, young

B. Suggestions
1. Seven, white, green
2. happy, young
3. warm, sunny, comfortable
4. old, rare

C.
1. happy, good, her, old
2. long, impressive, those
3. young, lavender, chiffon, lavender, satin
4. bright, spring (adjectival), lavender, purple
5. wooden, huge, silver, delicious
6. tall, handsome, dazed, his
7. that, pale, frazzled, his, new, father-in-law's (adjectival phrase)

Unit 6, page 28

A.
1. morning, quickly, loudly
2. so, often, today, painfully
3. soon, almost
4. immediately, too
5. really, too
6. slowly, afternoon, not, early,
7. more quickly, easily

B. Suggestions
1. most
2. very, yesterday
3. slowly, quietly
4. very, well

C.
1. quite
2. too, daringly
3. morning, very, very
4. silently, slowly, now
5. really, thoroughly
6. softly, morning, truly, firmly
7. now, somewhat, clearly

Unit 7, page 30

A.

1. *in* the drawer, *on* the right-hand side
2. *of* house, *in*
3. *underneath* the tree, *with* five kittens
4. *of* silk, *in* the fashion show
5. *of* milk, *of* sugar, *of* coffee
6. *for, below* the window
7. *to* Daphne, *in* his back pocket

B. Suggestions

1. at, on
2. for, in
3. in, of
4. Beyond, of

C.

1. *Under* the table, *of* five, *of* mischief
2. *during* the day, *within* the family
3. *Under* the circumstances, *about* his naughty son
4. *at* a company, *with* its headquarters, *in* a northern province, *of* Canada
5. *Outside* his interest, *in* work, *for* his child
6. *beneath* a somewhat gruff exterior, *to* himself
7. *into* the driveway, *about* 8:00, *through* the door, *by* 8:10

Unit 8, page 33

A.

1. but	5. When
2. or	6. until
3. however	7. both—and
4. Since	

B. Suggestions

1. If, and	3. or
2. Neither—nor, but	4. until

C.

1. both—and, but
2. if, however
3. Although, and
4. nevertheless, and

5. Neither—nor, so
6. Since, and
7. therefore

Unit 9, page 37

A.

1. Be careful!
2. Ouch!
3. Please watch your step!
4. no!

5. Your poem is excellent!
6. Look!
7. You must be mistaken!

Unit 10, page 38

A.

1. have eaten, Tr
2. can reach, Tr
3. will sign, Intr
4. wrote, Tr

5. rose, Intr
6. swims, Intr
7. consider, Tr

B.

1. hit, T
2. is, L
3. are, L
4. cooked, T

5. is, L
6. bought, T
7. seems, L

C.

1. I
2. Tr, DO—art history
3. L, PA—wrong
4. Tr, DO—children

5. I
6. L, PN—executive
7. L, PA—beautiful

D.

1. orders, T
2. appears, L
3. lasted, I
4. met, T

5. bought, T
6. were, L
7. are resting, I

Unit 11, page 43

A.

   1. a. check
       b. her

   2. a. steps
       b. them

   3. a. book
       b. Dick

   4. a. ball
       b. Ginny

   5. a. ride
       b. me

   6. a. Frisbee
       b. Diane

   7. a. news
       b. us

B.

1. us   5. Ruth
2. her   6. her
3. us   7. Mike
4. Aunt Lorena

C.

   1. a. Samuel
       b. class treasurer

   2. a. Tom Selleck
       b. fascinating

   3. a. you
       b. upstairs

   4. a. him
       b. King of the Realm

5. a. him
   b. recovered

6. a. baby
   b. crying

7. a. himself
   b. honest

D.

1. convincing
2. chairman
3. cooperative
4. outside

5. smiling
6. village president
7. exciting

Unit 12, page 46

A.

1.	P	5.	P
2.	A	6.	A
3.	A	7.	P
4.	P		

B.

1. A picnic in the park today will be had (by us).
2. A ham for sandwiches is being baked by Suzanne.
3. A huge bonfire has been planned by Les and Wes.
4. Many games are usually played by us.
5. We will also suggest swimming.
6. After the games, the women can serve dessert for everyone.
7. We will arrange transportation for the entire group.
8. The president has already mailed announcements for this special picnic.

C.

1.	A	5.	A
2.	P	6.	P
3.	A	7.	A
4.	P		

Unit 13, page 49

A.
1. killing
2. to give up, discouraging
3. whistling (the second one)
4. twisting, turning, to join
5. fallen, to do
6. shouting, to be
7. frightening, to react

B.
1. cutting out sweets
2. To be on time
3. thinking about his future, to become a lawyer
4. running a tight ship
5. jumping up and down, to hit the piñata
6. to cut your prices
7. Identifying your strengths and your weaknesses, to improve as a student

C. Suggestions
1. pealing
2. to cope
3. singing
4. To perform
5. to travel
6. Studying
7. charming

D.
1. raging
2. to ask, to do
3. Asking for help
4. enchanting, depressing
5. To listen quietly, amazing
6. Providing information, outstanding
7. fading, to return to their normal pursuits

Unit 14, page 53

A.
1. said, the
2. couples, heading . . . morning, went
3. swim, but
4. Apparently, the
5. tablecloth, napkins, silverware, and
6. Lessing, who . . . week, will
7. fish, Lonnie

B.
1. East; the
2. world; consequently,
3. control; they
4. ring; therefore,
5. disappointing; the
6. shrimp, soup, steak, and salad; they
7. roads, but . . . it; however,

C.
1. always, her . . . concise, clear, and critical.
2. Leann, her . . . editor, to . . . father.
3. house, but . . . months.
4. changed, we . . . outdoor theater.
5. health; consequently, . . . ulcers, strokes, or heart attacks.
6. Running daily, Dave . . . condition, exercised . . . time, and neighborhood; he . . . him.
7. Mayor Stockwell, stubborn . . . unconvinced, would . . . budget, regardless . . . criticism.

D.
1. vacation: Texas,
2. ingredients: flour,
3. "Dream Interpretation."
4. trait: honesty.
5. says, "This, . . . pass."
6. "tough."
7. "Reaction"; . . . "The Red Rose."

E.
1. person: artist, writer, and singer.
2. sheet: paper, pens, a ruler,
3. , "Could . . . today?"
4. book, be
5. day; therefore,
6. hand, the . . . honest, but
7. author, quiet . . . shy, has . . . admired: determination.

Unit 15, page 59

A.

1. one-track
2. two-hour
3. ex-wrestler
4. green-eyed
5. you're-in-this-with-me
6. chucky-chucky-choky
7. sixty-second

B.

1. extra-special asset—courtesy
2. student—although . . . City—
3. friends—not all at the same time, of course—
4. comfortable, loose-fitting clothes—in short,
5. "Abou Ben Adam"
6. Summerfest, a special . . . Chicago; friends—museums
7. quiet, gentle

C.

1. leaving—no, no—
2. (1837–1901) . . . social, economic,
3. come-and-get-it
4. pro-Nazi
5. *Titanic*
6. twenty-one
7. admire—honesty.

Unit 16, page 63

A.

1. Cl		5. Ph
2. Ph		6. Ph
3. Ph		7. Cl
4. Cl		

B.

1.	Ph	5.	Cl
2.	Cl	6.	Cl
3.	Ph	7.	Ph
4.	Ph		

C.

1.	D	5.	D
2.	D	6.	D
3.	I	7.	I
4.	I		

D.

1.	D	5.	D
2.	D	6.	I
3.	I	7.	I
4.	I		

Unit 17, page 66

A.

1.	CX	5.	CX
2.	C	6.	S
3.	S	7.	CC
4.	S		

B.

1.	S	5.	S
2.	CX	6.	S
3.	C	7.	C
4.	CX		

C.

1.	CX	5.	S
2.	S	6.	C
3.	C	7.	CX
4.	CC		

Unit 18, page 70
A.
1. I saw six uncut onions tossed into the salad.
2. Never serve pork that has not been cooked well to your family.
3. With two sprained wrists, Sonny couldn't drive to his school.
4. The chair with the velvet fringe was given to us by our aunt.
5. I saw her car that was stalled along the highway.
6. Sitting in the stands, we watched the active skaters.
7. Laughing, talking, and hugging, we enjoyed our reunion.

B.
1. Mrs. Stone eats greens beans only from the Farmer's Market.
2. The saleswoman with the long red hair knocked loudly on our door.
3. To prepare good food, you need fresh ingredients and time.
4. Kristen found her jacket thrown over the chair.
5. When our client was six, her mother died.
6. We saw three deer grazing along the edge of the road.
7. Rosa bowled a nearly perfect score.

Unit 19, page 75
A.

1.	CS	5.	SF
2.	SF	6.	CS
3.	CS	7.	SF
4.	CS		

B.

1.	RO	5.	RO
2.	CS	6.	RO
3.	CS	7.	RO
4.	RO		

C.

1.	CS & RO	5.	SF
2.	SF	6.	RO
3.	SF	7.	RO
4.	RO		

Unit 20, page 79

A.
1. What you have heard—noun clause
2. what they wanted to hear—noun clause
3. because she had burned her wrist—adverbial clause
4. that John sent—adjective (relative) clause
5. whichever tablecloth you prefer—noun clause
6. that Julie bought—adjective (relative) clause
7. When I left the house—adverbial clause

B.
1. While Dad slept—adverbial clause
2. that you wrote—adjective (relative) clause
3. what you ordered—noun clause
4. that you intend to introduce—adjective (relative) clause
5. What has just happened—noun clause
6. that Dan ordered—adjective (relative) clause
7. where you left them yesterday—adverbial clause

C.
1. who have temper tantrums—restrictive—no punctuation needed
2. whether you think so or not—nonrestrictive; call, whether
3. which . . . oven—nonrestrictive; bread, which . . . oven,
4. which Molly prepared—restrictive—no punctuation needed
5. That you have chosen this course of action—restrictive—no punctuation needed
6. whom you met last week—nonrestrictive—Jackdaw, whom . . . week,
7. that Amy covets—restrictive—no punctuation needed

D.
1. who bite strangers—restrictive—no punctuation needed
2. which won first prize at the Garden Club Show—nonrestrictive—flowers, which . . . Show,
3. why you left the meeting last Sunday—restrictive—no punctuation needed
4. whom you wish to believe—restrictive—no punctuation needed
5. When you're tense—nonrestrictive—tense, a
6. why you were there—restrictive—no punctuation needed
7. who studied music in Billings—nonrestrictive—Mother, who . . . Billings,

Unit 21, page 83

A.
1. two independent clauses—coordination
2. dependent—independent—subordination
3. independent—dependent—subordination
4. independent—dependent—subordination
5. dependent—independent—subordination
6. two independent clauses—coordination
7. independent—dependent—subordination

B.

Student's Choice

C.
1. dependent—independent—dependent—subordination
2. independent—dependent—independent—dependent—coordination and subordination
3. dependent—independent—subordination
4. independent—dependent—subordination
5. dependent—independent—dependent—subordination
6. two independent clauses—coordination
7. independent—independent—dependent—coordination and subordination

Unit 22, page 86

A.

1. taking long hikes
2. washing
3. to take a swim
4. mature, experienced
5. and well-mannered
6. drop "is" before creative
7. add "who" before the third "is" or write: who is honest, reliable, and Republican.

B.

1. drop "fire" and "it"
2. to develop
3. drink neither
4. and shopping
5. but simply tolerated by the voters
6. but writing stories
7. Mother warned us that there was danger at the quarry, *or* quarry and the serious trouble we could get into . . .

C.

1. was there
2. Mother served them a bowl of soup.
3. was rude
4. After Mr. Segal had criticized the new film so extensively,
5. but the teacher stopped him.
6. the students are still unsure
7. we went out

Answer Key: Post-Test

Exercise 1
    a. summer, students, directions, classes, fun, jobs, dreams
    b. families, time, opportunities, experiences, travel

Exercise 2
    a. formations, foliage
    b. boat (or excursion boat)
    c. coastline
    d. chefs, stewards
    e. passengers, waters

Exercise 3
    a. She, each, that, no one, his, her, which, those
    b. They, me, them, their

Exercise 4
    a. were flying, taking, staying, left
    b. have traveled, have been
    c. intend, will explore

Exercise 5
    a. Bob's, large, impressive, international, strongest
    b. lengthy, foreign, difficult, wise, careful, rewarding, his

Exercise 6
    a. fairly, very
    b. early, usually (extra credit for *at ten o'clock*)
    c. quite, truly
    d. always, daringly
    e. not, fiercely
    f. really, later

Exercise 7

a. for, in the library, for that math test, at noon
b. Under . . . circumstances, of Jem's . . . ability, in a sensible way
c. for a test, in the classroom, on the desk
d. between his . . . soda
e. Underneath . . . exterior

Exercise 8

a. Both—and, and
b. When, because
c. therefore, and
d. Since, and
e. Neither—nor, but

Exercise 9

a. Look this way, Brent!
b. Wait!
c. yes!
d. They're perfect!

Exercise 10

a. Swinging her feet over the edge of the pool, of the Hollywood scene
b. To tell the truth, by her poor judgment
c. by advice, given from inexperienced friends, to control her decisions
d. acting in films
e. Performing on stage, for years, growing up in a small town

Exercise 11

a. Cl
b. Ph
c. Cl
d. Cl
e. Ph
f. Cl

Exercise 12
    a. I
    b. D
    c. I
    d. D

Exercise 13
    a. Intr
    b. L
    c. Tr
    d. L
    e. Intr
    f. Tr

Exercise 14
    a. knew—had
    b. The teacher put the test in his hand

Exercise 15
    a. delighted—P; to stay up—Inf
    b. Opening his presents—G
    c. To please him—Inf, chosen—P
    d. building castles blocks—G
    e. to help him—Inf
    f. pleased—P

Exercise 16
    a. S—shadows
         V—loomed
    b. S—gusts
         V—made

    a. her
    b. solution

    a. me
    b. us

    a. ghost town—PN
    b. frightening—PA

Exercise 17
    a. As we walked
    b. Near the blazing fire, we
    c. you need skill . . . fire.
    d. While we were singing,
    e. immense hanging low

Exercise 18
    a. S
    b. CX
    c. CX
    d. C
    e. CC
    f. S

Exercise 19
    a. A
    b. P
    c. A
    d. P
    e. A
    f. A

Exercise 20
    a. talented, and cooperative
    b. dancing, and training . . .

Exercise 21
    a. When . . . sounded, the children
    b. The youngsters played ball, raced **around, and played on the** swings. (one possibility)

Exercise 22

- a. F
- b. CS
- c. RO
- d. F
- e. CS/RO
- f. RO

Exercise 23

- a. program; we . . . help.
- b. Jenna, Julie, and Jackson, but . . . soon.
- c. It's . . . Mike's schedule so.
- d. Friday, . . . us.
- e. effort; therefore, . . . participation.
- f. tomorrow, and . . . way.

Exercise 24

- a. A topic sentence introduces the idea of a paragraph.
- b. A thesis statement presents the major idea of a paper (essay, etc.).